Be a Greener Parent

This book is for Isla Joi and all the other children who need us big folk to make the change.

Teach®
Yourself

Be a Greener Parent
Lynoa Cattanach

For UK order enquiries: please contact Bookpoint Ltd,
130 Milton Park, Abingdon, Oxon, OX14 4SB.
Telephone: +44 (0) 1235 827720. Fax: +44 (0) 1235 400454.
Lines are open 09.00–17.00, Monday to Saturday, with a 24-hour
message answering service. Details about our titles and how to
order are available at www.teachyourself.co.uk

For USA order enquiries: please contact McGraw-Hill Customer
Services, PO Box 545, Blacklick, OH 43004-0545, USA.
Telephone: 1-800-722-4726. Fax: 1-614-755-5645.

For Canada order enquiries: please contact McGraw-Hill
Ryerson Ltd, 300 Water St, Whitby, Ontario, L1N 9B6, Canada.
Telephone: 905 430 5000. Fax: 905 430 5020.

Long renowned as the authoritative source for self-guided
learning – with more than 50 million copies sold worldwide –
the *Teach Yourself* series includes over 500 titles in the fields of
languages, crafts, hobbies, business, computing and education.

British Library Cataloguing in Publication Data: a catalogue record
for this title is available from the British Library.

Library of Congress Catalog Card Number: on file.

First published in UK 2007 by Hodder Education, part of
Hachette UK, 338 Euston Road, London NW1 3BH.

First published in US 2007 by The McGraw-Hill Companies, Inc.

This edition published 2007.

The *Teach Yourself* name is a registered trade mark of
Hodder Headline.

Typeset by MPS Limited, a Macmillan Company.

Printed in Great Britain for Hodder Education, a division of Hodder
Headline, an Hachette UK Company, 338 Euston Road, London
NW1 3BH, by Cox & Wyman Ltd, Reading, Berkshire RG1 8EX.

Acknowledgements

Thank you to Hayley and Alicia for helping out, but most of all to MJC for everything.

Image credits

Front cover: © Digifoto Silver/Alamy

Back cover: © Jakub Semeniuk/iStockphoto.com, © Royalty-Free/Corbis, © agencyby/iStockphoto.com, © Andy Cook/iStockphoto.com, © Christopher Ewing/iStockphoto.com, © zebicho – Fotolia.com, © Geoffrey Holman/iStockphoto.com, © Photodisc/Getty Images, © James C. Pruitt/iStockphoto.com, © Mohamed Saber – Fotolia.com

Contents

Foreword

If you are reading this book there is a high likelihood that you or someone close to you is going through the same thing as millions of other women in the world right now: pregnancy. Congratulations! The creation of a new life is one of the most amazing, precious and beautiful things we humans can experience. Unfortunately, as with many other things that fascinate or enrich us in our lives, we have taken parenting to excess. Our pregnancies, births and parenting are often over the top exercises in consumerism. Not only are we putting a big dent in our pockets, we are harming our health, environment, society and inevitably our children's future. In a bid to give our children the best of everything, we are actually becoming victims of mass-market media.

As you are reading this book it is probable that you are looking to do things differently because you wish to explore the world of green parenting. So, what is green parenting?

What is green?

The term 'green' was coined by the German Green Party when they contested their first national level election in 1980. Since then it has moved on a lot and most people readily identify with it. When applied to parenting, green means having an understanding of the environment and our society as a whole, and knowing how to boost health and vitality, naturally and holistically.

Gone are the days when green conjured up images of hippies and middle-class eccentrics. Green is for everyone. It affects everybody's lifestyle. As governments begin to wake up and take action against global warming, carbon emissions, burgeoning landfill sites, lifestyle-related health problems and the looming energy crisis we will all inevitably have to make lifestyle changes. Contrary to what some people say, this isn't necessarily the beginning of the end but simply another step in human evolution. This book is designed to be a simple step-by-step guide for those who want to start making changes for themselves and their family. It will help you prioritize which aspects of green parenting are most important to you and how much of it you can reasonably fit into your lifestyle. It will then give you practical guidance about how to make these changes and where to look for further information.

No matter what your circumstances, there are lots of little things you can incorporate into your lifestyle which won't involve an entire green household revolution. The suggestions in this book take busy lifestyles into consideration as well as introducing new concepts to those who would like to take green parenting a step further.

You will be taken on an informative green journey from conception, pregnancy and birth, right through to keeping a greener household for you and your family. The best news is that in the process of doing your bit for the planet, you will also be saving your hard-earned cash. This brings us onto the next big question: why go green anyway?

Why go green?

As a parent-to-be, you will be inundated with clinical information and mass-market publications disguised as free information guides and trial packs when actually they are just cunning marketing tools to get you to part with your money. Although some of this information is helpful it can also be overwhelming, so it's always best to look at all the options before making any decisions. Midwifes and health professionals are often rushed off their feet and may not be trained to answer questions about complementary treatments for common childhood ailments or where you can find a nursery that is cloth nappy (diaper) friendly. Thankfully this situation is starting to change as midwives are now being given a broader training. Everyone has the right to make their own choices. You can only make truly informed decisions that are right for you and your child when you are armed with all the facts. Informed decisions put you in control of your money and your lifestyle.

ENVIRONMENTAL BENEFITS

Did you know that approximately 8 million disposable nappies are thrown away in the UK every day? Every one of these nappies is dumped in a landfill site, many with the solid contents still inside them! These will sit in this landfill site for hundreds of years, as at least 10 per cent of every nappy is not biodegradable. Ten per cent of 8 million nappies a day amounts to a very large and ever-growing mountain of plastic. Local authorities are so concerned about reducing the amount of rubbish which goes to landfill sites that many run cloth nappy incentive schemes as part of their recycling campaigns.

Did you know that most household cleaners, textiles, paints and personal healthcare products contain chemicals untested for their toxicity to humans in combination with each other? Our bodies are contaminated with a cocktail of synthetic chemicals. In the past 50 years, approximately 80,000 new synthetic chemicals have been released into our environment.

Some of the products that we take for granted use up a disproportionate amount of resources and energy in their production. Many products are flown in from abroad contributing to carbon emissions and the greenhouse effect. Our lifestyles are putting a huge strain on our environment and energy supplies, which is reflected in our increasing energy bills.

Small changes to the products we consume, the services we use and our lifestyle can make a small but relevant impact on our environment. Starting to recycle your glass may seem irrelevant but it is an important link in a huge chain of long-term change.

SOCIAL BENEFITS

Choosing to buy nationally or locally produced items supports your national and local economy. British farmers have recently struggled due to the import of cheaper food from overseas and most rely on subsidies to boost their income. Many local companies are social enterprises or businesses with environmentally, ethically or socially led aims. Governments are now realizing the importance of social enterprise as an important element of British business and a means of stimulating a flagging economy.

Choosing to buy fair trade ensures the people who produced it have good working conditions and receive a fair proportion of the overall profit. Often fair trade products come from developing countries and their production has arisen through the setting up of a social initiative designed to empower the local people. When you pick up that fair trade chocolate bar, just think that you may be helping a mother in Ecuador support her family without being exploited.

When we walk down our local high street we are often faced with a plethora of big brand name shops interspersed with disused shop units which were once inhabited by local independent retailers. Small local companies find it hard to compete with the big boys and as a result are forced out of business. How many of us now find that we are forced to go to the supermarket for groceries rather than our local high street? The only way to ensure that the life and vibrancy of our communities continues is to support local products and services wherever possible.

HEALTH BENEFITS

The media is full of news about diet and lifestyle-related illnesses such as heart disease, obesity and cancer. More people than ever suffer from skin and respiratory ailments such as allergies, asthma and eczema. While some research has conclusively proven links between what we consume and our health, research on the link between what we inhale from our environment and what is absorbed through our skin is less clear. However, there is some evidence to suggest that the cocktail of chemicals we subject ourselves to through our household and personal hygiene products may be contributing to some ailments. Bear in mind that we don't actually need to smell like bubblegum or peaches to be clean and healthy, so it would often be better to be on the safe side and if in doubt leave it out. Being in control of your chemical environment is an important step towards a healthy start for your children.

MONEY MATTERS

Many people think that going green means lots of initial investment or buying premium products at high prices, but you can actually save money by being a greener parent. Prioritize your needs, recycle and share costs with others in your community and you could save thousands. Just by breastfeeding and using cloth nappies alone you could save approximately £1,500 (US$3,000) over two years. Change your banking and investment to a more ethical financial organization where you will receive more sympathetic charges and service and have peace of mind knowing your money is not being invested in anything unethical such as genetic engineering or the trade of weapons. In fact, some banks will even donate a proportion of their profits to charities of your choice so you can be charitable without lifting a finger.

We all know that the practical little changes we make at home are a small step towards changing our environment and the world as a whole. However, don't forget that emotional changes will also make a difference to how we relate and connect not only with our own family but also to our environment and community as a whole. This book touches on family relationships, work and life balance and the significant role of partners, family and friends throughout the various chapters, as these form an integral part of being a green parent.

Just remember, every little helps no matter how small. Dare to be different, set a standard and stand up for what you believe in!

How to use this book

You'll find everything to do with all things green in the pages of this book but you won't find any high-brow preaching. Green choices should be fun, practical, accessible and as cheap and convenient as possible. Being a green parent and making the necessary changes needn't mean a drastic lifestyle change. You will not need to boil wash cloth nappies in a big pot and sell the car in exchange for a cart horse (unless you want to of course).

PRIORITIZING NEEDS

Each chapter outlines different aspects of green parenting and contains lots of information to help you establish what changes are best for you and your family.

GREEN PARENT GUIDE

To help decide what suits you best you'll find a green parent guide at the end of each chapter. It is split into three sections: the first is for those who would like to start off making small, convenient and cost-effective changes; the second is for people who'd like to do all they reasonably can within the limits of their lifestyle and budget; the third is for those wanting to make big changes and really invest in their green choices. Simply choose the green category that best describes you (below) then read the tips for your chosen box in every chapter. Whether it's a cure for sore nipples or a source of organic tipples, you'll find easy solutions and helpful advice throughout this book.

Green parent guide

🍃 I'd like to keep things as convenient and easy as possible but I'd also like to save money and do the best I can for my family.

(Contd)

🍃🍃 I'm worried by what I hear on the news about things like food, health and the environment. I'd like to know more about these issues and the natural options available to me and my family. I'd like to do what I can but it has to be convenient.

🍃🍃🍃 I already reuse and recycle where possible. I'm aware of environmental and ethical issues and want easier access to the information I need to do as much as I can for my family and the environment.

FACT BOXES

Some of the chapters feature information boxes containing facts to help you make more educated decisions about what is right for you. This is a self-help guide not a manifesto, so don't worry, these are just a few basics to keep you informed!

INSIGHT BOXES

These feature green tips to help make green parenting easier.

The information in this book is relevant to everyone expecting the arrival of a child in their lives. Whether you are a prospective grandparent, godparent or adoptive parent, your primary interest is the same: obtaining the best for the babies and children you love. Please note that the pronouns used in this book when discussing children alternate between 'he' and 'she'. This is for convenience only and not because the issues that are being discussed are gender specific. Equally, you will find that this book addresses 'you' the reader, and sometimes assumes that 'you' are a mum-to-be. Again, this is for convenience only, and I hope that everyone reading this book feels included in its advice. The green parenting community welcomes you!

To know that even one life has breathed easier because you have lived, that is to have succeeded.

Ralph Waldo Emerson

1

Pregnancy and conception

In this chapter you will learn:
- *about naturally maximizing the chances of conception*
- *how to stay healthy during pregnancy*
- *how to cope with pregnancy gripes*
- *how partners can help out too.*

The whole baby thing is a completely different experience for every individual. Different races, religions, cultures and genders all have their own take on how to parent and what it means to be a parent. Whether it's your first time, whether the pregnancy is planned or unplanned, whether you're single or have a partner, hetero, or gay, having a baby is probably one of the most amazing things you'll ever do, so why not get you and your family off to the most healthy and practical start possible.

A green pregnancy involves dealing with issues of mental and physical health in the most natural and practical way possible. The experience of pregnancy varies so much from woman to woman that it is impossible to accurately give a picture of what to expect. Whether an expectant mother is the picture of blooming vitality or feels like a sack of potatoes with the IQ of a small rodent, sharing thoughts, ideas and feelings with other mums will be the best help and the biggest support. Pregnancy can be a rollercoaster of hormones, but keeping yourself informed and planning and prioritizing your needs will help you to keep calm about the pregnancy and be as naturally healthy as possible.

Preparing for conception

Try to ensure that as a couple you are both in tip top condition both mentally and physically. This may seem like pretty basic advice but we often don't realize just how much of an impact our lifestyles have on our bodies.

SUPPLEMENTS

Folic acid (vitamin B9) is recommended for mothers by health professionals before they conceive and for the first 12 weeks of pregnancy. Folic acid is a very important aid to the healthy development of a foetus. It can reduce the risk of defects such as spina bifida. People who are particularly low in zinc, iron and vitamin C may also wish to boost their diet with supplements, but it's a good idea to absorb vitamins and minerals through eating the appropriate foods. The information below is a rough guide to which foods are a natural resource of folic acid, zinc, iron, vitamin C, and omega-3 fatty acids. They will all help contribute to health and hopefully conception too.

Folic acid	Kiwi fruit, dried beans, peas, lentils, orange juice, oranges, dark leafy greens, soy nuts, avocados, broccoli, asparagus
Iron	Meat, seafood, prune juice, dry beans, wheat germ, oatmeal, tofu, soy nuts, grains
Zinc	Dairy products, beans and lentils, yeast, nuts, seeds and wholegrain cereals, pumpkin seeds, red meat
Vitamin C	Citrus fruits and juices, strawberries, bell peppers, tomatoes, dark leafy greens, broccoli, brussel sprouts
Omega-3 fatty acids	Salmon, walnuts, flaxseed, leafy green vegetables

DIET

This affects our vitality, health and well-being, both mental and physical. It can even affect your chances of conceiving and some foods are believed to be powerful aphrodisiacs. The most common sense advice regarding diet is for mothers to limit their coffee, tea and alcohol intake, completely eliminating them if possible (except perhaps for the odd glass of wine). Try some herbal teas and malt drinks instead. Cut down on dairy and meat products, balancing your diet with plenty of nuts, seeds and pulses. These are a great source of omega-3 and other Essential Fatty Acids (EFAs) which contribute to the healthy development of the foetus. Try to buy organic when possible (see Chapter 4 for more information). If you are a vegan or vegetarian make sure that you boost your protein and calcium intake. Cut down on fat and refined sugar intake and avoid food additives (for more information about food additives see Chapter 4). Make sure you help your body cleanse itself and absorb as much of the nutrients you put into it as possible by drinking at least two to three litres of water per day. The table below is a rough guide to some conception super foods.

Fertility male	Oysters have a super high zinc content. Zinc is critical for maintaining optimum semen volume and blood testosterone levels in men. Foods which contain lots of vitamin E, such as wheat germ oil, dry roasted almonds, safflower oil, corn oil, turnips, leafy greens, raw mango, dry roasted peanuts, broccoli, kiwi and spinach, can improve sperm mobility and viability.
Fertility female	There seems to be no particular food for women which boosts fertility. However, being extremely underweight or overweight can affect female fertility as can high levels of salt, caffeine, nicotine and alcohol. Women who are trying to conceive should also avoid artificial sweeteners. Some research suggests that consuming large amounts of tofu may affect fertility so if you're vegetarian or vegan, try to balance the amount of tofu you eat with other sources of protein.
Libido	Celery, raw oysters, bananas, avocados, almonds, peaches, strawberries, eggs, liver, figs, garlic, chocolate.

Detoxifying	Beetroots, radishes, artichokes, cabbage, broccoli, sesame seeds, spirulina, chlorella, seaweed, green tea, green leafy vegetables, lemons, watercress and garlic.

> **Insight**
>
> Men should get 15 mg of zinc and at least 1,000 mg of calcium daily, and eat foods rich in vitamin E such as olive oil and wheat germ. Both men and women should avoid alcohol, caffeine and smoking.

EXERCISE

This is essential. If you already have a pretty hectic exercise regime consider toning it down a little or swapping some high impact activities for a yoga or pilates session. If you're not already exercising why not get fit gently with swimming, yoga, pilates, walking or Tai chi. Studies have shown that obesity and high blood pressure can affect fertility so it's worth making sure you give yourself an MOT and your circulation a boost.

REST

Sleep deals with stress and helps our bodies to rejuvenate for the day ahead. Make sure that as a couple you both get at least 8 hours sleep per night.

> **Insight**
>
> Remember, eight hours' sleep per night – each! Even if this means missing a favourite TV programme.

Try to make sure that you and your partner are as relaxed as possible and if there's stress in your life, try to minimize it. Everyone needs a bit of time to themselves, even if it is only ten minutes. Relax and be by yourself, go for a walk, retreat to your bedroom and read a book or simply daydream. If you really want to go for it, try meditation. You can have music and candles as added extras but they are by no means essential to relaxation. When spending time with your partner, play a game together or read and don't forget the radio. There are some really great plays, music and comedy on this all too often forgotten medium.

COMMUNICATION

This can be through speech, touch and deed and it is an important part of any relationship. Try to make sure that through your communication you stay in tune with each other's needs, hopes and fears. Chatting things through after a hard day at work and showing that you empathize with each other can help. Listen to each other. You'll feel closer. Take time to give or receive a quick neck massage or even just an unexpected hug to help you both feel relaxed and united. Help each other out with little chores around the house and treat your partner by arranging a surprise.

TOXINS

Remove these from your lifestyle wherever possible. This includes the toiletries and cosmetics you both use, the cleaning products used around the house, furnishings and decoration, air pollution, noise pollution and food. Research has indicated that certain environmental and household pollutants can affect fertility. The research may or may not be definitive but why expose yourselves to a barrage of chemicals which cost you a lot of money when you can live just as happily and healthily without them?

Make sure you don't have central heating too high and air your house regularly. Spider plants are the best household plants to clean the air. Not only are they easy to keep but also act as natural filters, absorbing chemicals found around the house such as formaldehyde, benzene and trichloroethylene and reducing their concentration by up to 90 per cent. Plants can also remove other contaminants such as cigarette smoke, carbon monoxide, harmful viruses and bacteria, as well as mould spores. Don't forget to switch off computers, monitors and any other electrical appliances on standby. Not only will you save money and cut energy use but you will also reduce another kind of pollution in the home, electro-magnetic field pollution or EMFs. For more information about EMFs and reducing and avoiding other toxins in your life see Chapter 10.

RESEARCH

Knowledge is power and the better informed you are the more empowered you'll feel.

PRE-CONCEPTION PLANS AND NATURAL FERTILITY TREATMENT

These ensure that conception happens as quickly and as naturally as possible. Pre-conception plans involve implementing a four- to six-month plan for both partners based around an organic diet designed by a specialist. The diet is derived from a series of nutritional tests and helps the body get rid of toxins and go back to optimum health. It may also involve specific forms of exercise, complementary treatments such as acupuncture or cranio-sacral therapy and the use of homeopathic or herbal preparations.

Natural fertility treatments may also involve monitoring a woman's menstrual cycle, temperature and changes in vaginal discharge and cervix to determine when she is most fertile. These methods can be self-taught and used at home rather than buying an over the counter ovulation test kit. You can find lots of advice in books and on the Internet about how to naturally determine when ovulation occurs. Alternatively, ask your doctor for some advice, as many now provide this type of information or can point you in the right direction.

CONCEPTION PROBLEMS

These can arise through stress, diet, past contraception methods, age, hormonal problems, smoking, alcohol and obesity. You've probably heard reports in the news of dropping male sperm counts due to toxins and pesticides in drinking water and general lifestyle. That's why it's important to give yourself a head start by sorting out your diet and immediate environment in preparation for conception as soon as you can.

If you have been trying to get pregnant without success the important thing is to stay calm. When a couple are actively trying to conceive, the stress and pressure they put on themselves can often delay things. Generally, if you have been trying to conceive without success for a year or more you will be diagnosed with having fertility problems.

There are a number of clinics which deal naturally and sympathetically with conception issues using diet, lifestyle and complimentary therapies as well as visualization and exercise techniques. Alternatively, contact your local therapy centre, as herbalism, acupuncture and naturopathy have all been shown to aid conception. For more information about the various therapies available see Chapter 7.

Pregnancy

Pregnancy, especially if it's the first time, is an incredible experience. This doesn't just apply to the mother either. For partners too, nothing can completely prepare them for the coming nine months. Almost all of the suggestions given here are equally applicable to the partner!

Make sure that you respect the fact that there is another human being growing inside you and treat your body accordingly. Many of the same rules for diet and exercise during the time when you are trying to conceive can be applied during pregnancy. You will go through many different phases in your pregnancy and many women swing from feeling great to feeling rundown. No matter how you feel, please remember that it's all natural and that if you're ever unsure never be scared to ask your midwife or doctor. All too often in modern medicine we get swept along with a tide of information and a certain way of doing things. While this medical information is essential and useful, there is always more than one way to look at an issue.

Insight

It is your right to question your midwife or any other health professional until you feel confident. You're paying for this service so go for it! Remember that knowledge will help you make your own informed decisions.

Arm yourself with a good book which details the different stages of pregnancy and the various issues you may encounter. If you can afford it, try attending Active Birth classes, with your partner if possible. These classes are designed to inform you about pregnancy and birth and the more natural ways to do it. The aim of Active Birth classes is to put you in control of the birth of your child through adopting the most natural methods of birthing, from massage to birth positions. You and your partner will learn how to massage and breathe effectively in order to naturally aid the different stages of labour. You will also be taught about side effects of all the drugs you'll be offered at the hospital.

Being knowledgeable about what is happening to you and your baby will help you to ask the health professionals the right questions, as well as putting you more in control of your pregnancy and birth. Obsessing and being overcautious about a pregnancy can be just as bad as ignorance so try to keep yourself healthily informed without overdoing it and causing unnecessary stress. Please remember that being green is really about practicality and a healthy future, so just do what you want to do and be who you want to be. Being a 'green parent' doesn't need to be a way of life unless you want it to be. Every little counts.

EARLY PREGNANCY, PROBLEMS AND NATURAL SOLUTIONS

Where possible, try to treat routine ailments and niggles as naturally as possible and avoid antibiotics unless completely necessary. They can upset the delicate balance of the already hormonal body and lead to thrush. It's always a good idea to use a health professional for an accurate diagnosis if need be and then you can treat the ailment using natural remedies, only resolving to use pharmaceuticals if absolutely necessary. For more information on all the major complimentary therapies available please see Chapter 7. Natural remedies for the major pregnancy niggles can be found over the next few pages. You may not need any of these as a woman's body has a natural way of keeping itself healthy during pregnancy. Remember that your partner may suffer sympathetic pregnancy symptoms to yours and can also be treated using the same remedies.

Natural or complimentary therapies work in harmony with the body's natural healing mechanisms to aid and maximize the body's ability to recover naturally from minor ailments. The benefit of using these remedies is that, if used correctly, they have no dangerous side effects. Complimentary remedies work on a holistic basis. This means that they work in combination with general health, mental health, diet and exercise. Therefore each individual will react slightly differently to different treatments. It is wise to consult a skilled and registered practitioner for guidance alongside your doctor and birth consultants.

Backache
Cause: an increase in weight and change in shape.

Natural solutions:

- *yoga and pilates can help you maintain better posture – try to avoid an arch in your lower back when standing by keeping your bottom tucked under and your shoulders straight but relaxed*
- *good shoes and an insole if necessary can help correct posture*
- *aromatherapy massage – a combination of rose, geranium, lavender and roman chamomile combined with base oil*
- *osteopathy*
- *acupuncture*
- *aromatherapy*
- *homeopathy.*

Constipation
Cause: pressure on the bowel due to the baby's weight and shape.

Natural solutions:

▶ *homeopathy*
▶ *avoid wheat, eat more dried fruit, drink plenty fluids, drink red raspberry leaf tea (only in the last month of pregnancy).*

Piles
Cause: can be brought on by constipation or stress and lack of nutrients.

Natural solutions: ice cold witch hazel compress.

Thrush
Cause: change in hormones; use of routine antibiotics; immune system required to work harder during pregnancy.

Natural solutions:

▶ *homeopathy*
▶ *chamomile, fennel or thyme vaginal compress, eat natural yoghurt and lots of raw foods, garlic, olive oil massaged into labia vulva, tea tree oil*
▶ *wear cotton underwear and loose clothing*
▶ *avoid all kinds of sugars including honey and molasses.*

Exhaustion
Cause: hormonal changes and state of mind.

Natural solutions:

▶ *shiatsu*
▶ *aromatherapy (put a few drops of ylang ylang, jasmine or lavender in the bath)*

- ▶ *exercise, especially swimming or yoga, can energize but equally ensure a good night's sleep (but avoid evening classes for maximum effect)*
- ▶ *homeopathy.*

Anaemia

Cause: increased nutritional needs required to grow and sustain two systems.

Natural solutions:

- ▶ *homeopathy*
- ▶ *drink nettle tea, red raspberry leaf tea (only at the end of pregnancy); eat iron-rich foods such watercress, pumpkin seeds and oats; vitamin C is also needed to help the body break iron down into a useable form so be sure to compliment your iron-rich foods with lots of fruits and green vegetables.*

Pelvic pain

Cause: pressure on muscles and ligaments due to growing baby.

Natural solutions:

- ▶ *massage*
- ▶ *TENS – a Transcutaneous Electrical Nerve Stimulator (or TENS machine) delivers small electrical pulses to the body via electrodes placed on the skin. This is thought to help ease pain and seems to vary in effectiveness from person to person.*

Carpal tunnel syndrome

Cause: the swelling and fluid retention common during pregnancy can increase the pressure in the carpal tunnel, a bony canal formed by the wrist bones, compressing the nerve that runs through it. Symptoms may include numbness, tingling, burning, pain or a dull ache in the fingers, hand, wrist and even up the arm to the shoulder. In severe and chronic cases, hands may also feel clumsy or weak.

Natural solutions:

- *avoid activity that requires forceful, repetitive hand movements*
- *wear wrist or hand braces while working – if working at a computer adjust the height of chairs so wrists aren't bent downward when typing, using a special ergonomic keyboard can help in some cases, and take breaks to stretch hands*
- *change sleeping position – prop up affected arms and avoid sleeping on hands, shake hands on waking to relieve pain or numbness*
- *yoga can help relieve the pain and increase hand strength.*

Stretch marks
Cause: stretching of the skin over your bump may cause visible marks (red at first turning to silver later) depending on how elastic your skin is.

Natural solutions:

- *aloe vera gel – directly from the leaf or a 100 per cent gel from a health food shop – applied to belly, hips and thighs*
- *zinc-rich foods such as pumpkin and hemp seeds can improve the skin's elasticity*
- *coconut and rose oil will moisturize your bump.*

Morning sickness
Cause: due to the change in hormones, the valves which control the flow of stomach juices become more elastic and don't work so effectively.

Natural solutions:

- *acupuncture*
- *shiatsu in the form of acupressure bracelets which can be bought from any large pharmacy or health food shops*

- *aromatherapy – a few drops of ginger or peppermint oil inhaled from a tissue may relieve the feeling of nausea*
- *homeopathy – Ipecac for continued nausea not relieved by vomiting; sepia if the nausea is made worse by the thought or smell of food; Nux Vomica for morning nausea; Pulsatilla for evening nausea; eat ginger and drink ginger tea; vitamin B6 found in bananas, cereals, lentils and fish.*

Heartburn and indigestion
Cause: as above and due to pressure exerted on the diaphragm by your baby.

Natural solutions:

- *chamomile tea, fennel tea, avoid rich spicy foods and alcohol*
- *yoga and pilates can aid posture and reduce pressure on diaphragm*
- *homeopathy.*

Bleeding gums
Cause: increased nutritional needs and changes in hormones.

Natural solutions: eat vitamin C-rich foods; drink red raspberry leaf tea (late pregnancy only).

Insomnia
Cause: hormonal changes; a baby which is active during the evening; general discomfort in late pregnancy.

Natural solutions:

- *aromatherapy – lavender, neroli and rose combined with a carrier oil and burned in a vaporizer*
- *chamomile tea drunk before bed can aid sleep*
- *homeopathy*
- *outdoor exercise*
- *a well-ventilated room; no TV before bed, read instead; unplug all electrical equipment in bedroom*

▶ *drink celery juice or warm water with honey and cider vinegar before bed.*

Fluid retention and swelling
Cause: due to hormonal changes, minerals in the blood cells may become unbalanced which can lead to swelling.

Natural solutions:

▶ *homeopathy – try Apis or Natrum Mur*
▶ *leg massage.*

Cramps
Cause: poor circulation; calcium deficiency may cause cramps in hands, calves, feet and thighs.

Natural solutions:

▶ *nettle tea for leg cramps, garlic incorporated into the diet on a regular basis*
▶ *homeopathy*
▶ *daily leg massage.*

Varicose veins
Cause: increased blood in body; increased pressure in leg veins due to extra weight and pressure on inferior vena cava.

Natural solutions: witch hazel compress; lemon juice compress.

Stress and mood swings
Cause: hormonal changes and/or mixed emotions regarding parenthood.

Natural solutions:

▶ *aromatherapy – geranium combined with jasmine oil is a natural mood enhancer (combine with a carrier oil and burn in a vaporizer)*

▶ *homeopathy*
▶ *exercise.*

DIET AND EXERCISES

These are even more important during pregnancy than they were during conception. You now have the opportunity to give your baby the best start in life by feeding it lots of healthy food to aid its development in the womb and by making sure that your baby's temporary accommodation (that'll be mum) is in the best condition possible. Stick to the diet tips mentioned for conception and women should also remember to continue taking folic acid supplements. Expectant mums should drink plenty of water and try some raspberry leaf tea in the last trimester which may aid labour. They should also avoid eating fatty and acidic foods.
As pregnancy progresses women may find themselves experiencing nausea and indigestion. Starting off with plenty of acid-free foods will help minimize this problem. Eating small amounts at regular intervals and avoiding processed meals will also help. Health professionals recommend that you should avoid soft and blue cheeses, patés and raw or soft-boiled eggs. Alcohol is allowed in very small amounts. One to two units, once or twice per week is plenty. Likewise caffeinated tea and coffee should be kept to a minimum and please, just don't do cigarettes or drugs. It's not worth it.

Try to do as much walking as possible during early pregnancy. Not only will you be keeping fit and healthy but you'll also be helping the environment by avoiding using a car and it's free! Being outdoors will also ensure that you get plenty of natural sunlight which is important for the healthy development of your baby's bones. Sunlight stimulates the production of vitamin D so it will help your hair, teeth, nails and bones stay in good condition too.

As your pregnancy progresses consider joining a prenatal yoga class. Yoga is a great way to prepare your body for birth and keep you relaxed. It is great to meet other mums to be too.

Pilates is a form of exercise which recognizes and targets the pelvic floor area and teaches you how to exercise your pelvic floor through subtle but controlled and targeted movements. Exercising your pelvic floor muscles in this way will help you to be stronger and more in control during the birth process but it will also help things pop back into shape quicker after the birth and ensure that you minimize the chances of bladder problems in the future. Aqua natal classes offer very gentle and relaxing exercise in the late stages of pregnancy. Some people believe that baby enjoys them too! Try to avoid high impact activities which would put pressure on the spine such as running (in later pregnancy), horse riding and trampolining.

Exercise and staying active is good but prospective mums should get plenty of rest and time to themselves as well. Try a nice relaxing warm bath but don't have it too hot. Avoid working beyond 28 weeks if you are feeling worn out or your work is strenuous. Don't be a martyr to the nine until five daily grind. Enjoy your pregnancy!

RELATING TO THE BABY INSIDE YOU

By the fourth month of pregnancy your baby will begin to hear sounds and by the sixth month your baby's eyes will open and she'll react when you touch your bump. It may be hard to imagine but it is possible to begin to form a bond with the baby inside you at this early stage.

Touching and massaging your bump with coconut oil, speaking and singing to your baby can all help to form a strong bond. Some studies have shown that babies relate to noises they have heard on a regular basis whilst in the womb when they are born and they may even have a calming effect. Try sleeping with a few of the clothes you plan to put on your baby when she is born. Not only will it ensure that any chemicals left on the fabric (see Chapter 8) have been removed but the clothes will have a familiar and calming smell for your baby.

MENTAL HEALTH DURING PREGNANCY

As mentioned before, pregnancy can be a bit of a rollercoaster for some people. One minute you are feeling like a voluptuous earth mother with a mane of shiny healthy hair and glowing skin. The next thing you know, you're sat on the sofa feeling like a spotty, greasy, sack of potatoes, crying at a daytime soap. This is fine, it's normal! Keeping active and having a healthy diet can help avoid the low times. Often we find ourselves moving house before the arrival of a new baby with none of our family and friends nearby. Try to ensure that you join some local groups or exercise classes. If money is an issue try your local community centre, library, doctor's surgery and hospital to see if there are any free or subsidized groups or activities. All hospitals offer antenatal classes but it's worth finding out if the hospital offers any other parenting classes or groups.

If you're feeling rundown why not treat yourself to a massage? If you can't afford one ask your partner or a willing friend. Treat yourself to a new hairstyle or some new beauty products. As mentioned previously, try to steer clear of chemicals, especially hair dyes. Use naturally derived plant hair dyes instead. There are lots of companies that offer chemical free toiletries and cosmetics. Have a look on the Internet or at the back of this book for more details.

If you're on a budget but still fancy treating yourself, try out the National Childbirth Trust nearly new sales. Their website or information line provides information about when the next sale in your area will be. You can pick up some great funky maternity clothes at these events as well as loads of other parenting goodies. Try charity shops and online swap and sell sites such as BabyGROE, eBay, gumtree, Freecycle and other parenting sites.

Buying second-hand clothes is a cheap, environmentally friendly and ethical way to be a practical funky mum and there's nothing like a few new clothes to cheer you up.

If things are really getting you down, make sure you talk to someone about it, as getting it off your chest really is the first step to feeling much better. Nowadays many families are scattered and often lack the support of a close knit community. Make an effort to make connections and you'll be surprised at how many people feel just like you.

A PARTNER'S GUIDE TO BEING PREGNANT

While many women are now deciding to go it alone as a single parent through choice or otherwise, a partner also deserves recognition in the pregnancy period. Although the woman carries the baby, the partner can often carry burdens too, such as financial concerns, housing issues and of course the concern about the mothers and the baby's health and well-being, not to mention worries about being a good parent.

As well as this there may be concerns about how a couple's relationship will change. As an expectant woman's hormones and moods fluctuate so too can the emotions within a loving relationship. This is all totally normal and there are ways to deal with all of these changes as constructively as possible.

Make sure you create time to spend together as a couple at least once a week. During this time you can discuss your hopes, fears and excitement for the future. Try to attend a pregnancy preparation class together such as an Active Birth class. It will help bring you together as much as possible as an expectant couple and give you all the information you need to deal with everything that pregnancy, birth and early parenting throw at you.

As a partner progresses in her pregnancy, try to inform yourself about the changes she is going through and help out where possible without getting in the way or treading on her toes. This will help prepare you for the extra mothering required by your partner when the baby is born. If you already have children make sure this help extends to them too. Not only will it strengthen the bonds between you and the other children, but it will help them to feel included and needed when the baby comes along.

Make plans for attending the birth (Active Birth classes are also useful for this) and speak to other partners who are preparing for a baby in order to obtain other perspectives. If you don't know any, get online. There are many online dad forums such as Fathers Direct, BabyGROE and the National Fatherhood Initiative. Remember that this is a shared experience and although a partner may not be going through the physical aspects of pregnancy and birth, many of the same pregnancy problems will crop up for them too. It is not unheard of for fathers to experience heartburn and swelling in sympathy with their partner. The same natural remedies apply!

Green parent guide to pregnancy and conception

🍃 Take up a gentle form of exercise. Drink plenty of water and cut out processed food from your diet. Avoid foods containing fat and refined sugar. Remember to take folic acid supplements and give your immune system a boost by eating plenty of fruit and vegetables and drinking at least two litres of water a day. Avoid cigarettes or drugs. Limit caffeine and alcohol intake. Try to avoid using harsh chemicals and cleaning agents around your home and keep it well ventilated. Make sure you take time out to keep yourself relaxed and spend time massaging, talking and singing to your bump.

🍃🍃 Eat foods high in folic acid, iron, zinc vitamin C and EFAs. Take time out to relax by yourself and with your partner. Add yoga, pilates or walking to your usual

(Contd)

exercise routine. Communicate both verbally and physically with your partner. Avoid toiletries and cosmetics containing chemicals. Try to treat routine pregnancy niggles with natural remedies. Attend NCT sales and visit charity shops for maternity wear. Have a pregnancy massage and attend an antenatal yoga class.

🌿🌿🌿 Buy organic fresh food. Monitor your menstrual cycle to determine your fertile periods. Put aside time to meditate and relax. Consider a pre-conception plan. Eradicate as many toxins as possible from your lifestyle. Eat as much organic and fair trade raw and sprouting vegetables and seeds as possible. Use natural oils for massage and burning. Attend Active Birth classes. Consult a registered complimentary health practitioner to instruct and guide you through the natural remedies for pregnancy. Buy British made, fair trade or organic maternity clothes. Continue regular meditation focusing on a natural easy birth.

2

Birth

In this chapter you will learn:
- *how to decide what type of birth is right for you*
- *what kind of help you would like with your birth*
- *how to prepare for as natural a birth as possible.*

Having a green birth really just means doing it as naturally as possible. You can have music, candles, incense and a birthing pool if that's what green means to you, or you can go for a birth at a hospital of your choice with as little intervention as possible. The decision is entirely yours and nobody is judging you on your efforts. Remember that your aim is to make this as healthy and enjoyable an experience as possible.

Planning a birth

Birthing is the most natural thing in the world, although it doesn't feel like it for everyone and that is in no way a personal failure. It is such a different and unique experience for every individual. While advances in medical science allow many more children to survive through infancy and beyond, women seem to have lost touch with their natural instinct to birth. We humans can only control nature up to a point and that's where medical science and natural instinct meet and, at times, clash.

Choosing to have a natural birth gives the privilege of having as much control as possible during the birth whilst also having the reassurance of fantastic medical facilities either in the birth centre, hospital or an ambulance ride away. Avoiding unnecessary drugs during birthing ensures that mother and baby are clear headed and that all the natural hormones for bonding, feeding and recovery are allowed to do what Mother Nature intended them to. Nature can only be managed up to a point, however, so it is important to prepare a birth plan but to have no expectations. Be open-minded and prepared for anything. Setting high expectations may lead to disappointment if plans change and remember that the safety of mother and child is paramount. Make sure that the decisions you make are ones you all feel safe and comfortable with.

When a pregnancy is confirmed with a doctor, mums-to-be are given an appointment for a check-up and scan. This is generally between 11 and 16 weeks, but it varies depending on which country you are living in. The scan will determine whether the pregnancy is progressing normally. If it isn't, the parents are informed and may be asked to make some pretty tough decisions about the future of their child. Scans can be inaccurate and some parents believe that no matter what is wrong with their child it still deserves to be born and supported. Some parents choose not to have a scan. The choice is completely yours but you will be advised by health professionals to have it. If it is a first child the awe of seeing your tiny baby bobbing around can really help you connect with the life growing inside.

At this time parents are also given a lot of clinical literature designed to help them understand the development and growth of the baby and to prepare for parenthood. Much of it will be produced by marketing companies independently or on behalf of the hospital and will be packed full of conventional advice and mass-market advertisements for products that aren't really needed. To be a good parent all you need to provide is love, warmth and food (breast milk if possible). Please don't feel pressurized into buying things. Just do what you think is best and buy what you really need not what you *think* you need!

Expectant mums are given a birth plan to fill out at this point. Whether birthing at home or hospital, it's a good idea to complete this so that no matter what happens, anyone assisting the birth will be clear about your wishes. To help you make informed decisions about birthing and what to include in a birth plan, here's a summary of the options available, both conventional and natural. However these are not exhaustive, so please get as informed as possible and consult any of the further reading suggested at the back of this book.

Tests, interventions and newborn treatments

These are routine throughout pregnancy and birth for both mother and child. There is much conflicting research as to the validity and the side effects of these treatments but every parent has the option to opt in or out. Preferences should be included in the birth plan but before making any decisions arm yourself with as much information as possible. It's all very well deciding to do everything as naturally as possible by opting out of certain tests, interventions and treatments but please be aware that you should be absolutely 100 per cent sure about your decision as any complications could lead to feelings of blame and guilt. To put you in the picture, the following pages provide a rough guide to the tests, interventions and treatments mother and baby will be offered, when they will occur, why, possible side effects and any natural alternatives available.

INTERNAL EXAMINATIONS

Internal examinations are common during labour in order to assess progress. They can be uncomfortable and invasive.

Natural alternatives:

▶ *During a natural healthy labour, fewer checks will be required.*
▶ *Make sure any checks are done between contractions and ask if they can be performed whilst standing up with a foot resting on a bed or a chair rather than lying down in order to reduce pain.*

INDUCTION

Induction takes place just before or during labour if labour is slow or baby is late. The extremely powerful contractions caused by induction may lead to the need for pain relief drugs and cause the baby to become stressed. Induction also requires foetal monitoring which may stress the mother and inhibit movement. An intervention like this may lead to others and a failed induction may result in a caesarean section.

Natural alternatives:

- *love-making – semen contains a hormone which softens the cervix*
- *exercise, especially yoga or walking*
- *an enema – castor oil (ask the birth attendant)*
- *a glass or two of wine, spicy food*
- *acupuncture*
- *cervical massage (ask birth attendant)*
- *nipple stimulation*
- *homeopathy*
- *herbal treatments such as black and blue cohosh and red raspberry leaf tea; three capsules of evening primrose oil daily for up to a week.*

FORCEPS OR VENTOUSE

This intervention involves the use of metal clamps or vacuum suction to help ease the baby out of the vagina. It may cause distress and discomfort to mother and child and may also cause compression of the skull and pressure on the spine.

Natural alternatives:

- *Assuming an active birth in an upright position or 'all fours' and avoiding drugs during labour should reduce the need for forceps or ventouse.*

ELECTRONIC FOETAL MONITORING (EFM)

EFM may be required to monitor the baby's heart rate and respiration levels during labour or late pregnancy testing. Unfortunately, incorrect reading of the results may lead to unnecessary intervention. EFM also restricts the mother's ability to move around, therefore stopping her from assuming optimum birthing positions.

Natural alternatives:

▶ *Continuous monitoring is usually only necessary if there have been health problems with mother or child or if there has been medical intervention, otherwise occasional monitoring is usually all that's required. Hand-held or wireless devices can be used to allow the mother freedom of movement.*

VITAMIN K DROPS (FOR YOUR BABY)

This treatment is offered within the first few weeks of life. This is because, while all mammals including human babies are born with low levels of vitamin K which helps blood clot, some infants are born with a disease which causes severe bleeding and others may develop it up to 12 weeks after they are born. It is believed that giving babies vitamin K will safeguard against fatalities among infants with this condition and it has also proven to be a deterrent against developing it.

However, there is speculation about vitamin K increasing the incidence of childhood leukaemia and other cancers. There is also the possibility of a higher incidence of jaundice.

Natural alternatives:

▶ *Mother should eat a sensible diet with plenty of vitamin K-rich foods such as green vegetables, alfalfa, kelp, green tea and a moderate amount of dairy products which will reduce the chances that the baby will be affected by this disease.*

PKU SCREENING (FOR YOUR BABY)

PKU screening may take place during infancy (normally within the first week) in order to make sure the baby doesn't have a condition called *Phenylketonuria* (inability to process amino acids, found in animal proteins and dairy products). If left untreated this condition can cause hyperactivity, eczema, convulsions and retarded mental development. The test is carried out by taking a blood sample from the baby's heel and may cause distress to the newborn.

Natural alternatives:

▶ *Some research has shown that taking the blood using the venipuncture method (a small needle inserted into the vein) causes less distress to the child, so ask a health practitioner to use this method and hold the baby closely while the procedure is carried out.*

EPISIOTOMY

Episiotomy occurs during labour and is the surgical enlargement of the vagina by making a small incision in the perineum (the bit of skin and muscle between the vagina and the anus). The procedure is uncomfortable and intrusive. Recovery can be painful with a risk of infection and can increase the chances of further tearing.

Natural alternatives:

▶ *Make a clear request to avoid episiotomy in the birth plan and to attendants and health professionals.*
▶ *Make sure plenty of foods containing protein, vitamin E and fatty acids, especially omega-3s are eaten during pregnancy.*
▶ *Take regular exercise including pelvic floor exercises (ask your midwife for more details).*
▶ *Practice perineal massage, especially in the last six weeks of pregnancy. Vitamin E oil or olive oil are good and are more*

effective if the massage is done right after having a bath as this helps soften the tissues.

▶ *Massage the perineum with oil during labour and use a warm compress to relax the tissues.*

▶ *Ask a birth attendant to perform perineal support (applying pressure to an overstretched perineum during labour).*

▶ *Take time over the second stage of labour and use a variety of birth positions.*

▶ *During birth use a hot compress on the perineum if it feels painful and overstretched.*

EPIDURAL

This is the most popular form of pain relief during labour, particularly when a caesarean section is required as it allows the mother to stay aware and clear-headed throughout the process without any sensation of pain.

Depending on dosage, this method can numb the mother from the waist down, therefore inhibiting movement and sensation and the ability to 'bear down' when required to push.

It inhibits the production of the hormone which stimulates labour and contractions thus increasing the risk of further interventions such as forceps, ventouse, labour-enhancing drugs and caesarean section. It may cause the newborn to be stressed and may effect its reflexes such as suckling.

Natural alternatives:

▶ *Epidural is best used only for emergency situations such as a caesarean section.*

▶ *Try to use other more natural forms of pain relief instead.*

Remember that medical institutions do like to stick to their routines. Only through more and more people asking for changes will they eventually begin to see the merit of different procedures so your opinion and your request are important.

Where to birth

There are basically four options, hospital, home or birth centre (possibly five if the birth happens unexpectedly in a public place!). There are pros and cons to each option and any choices made will depend on your own personal priorities or health issues.

HOSPITAL

This will offer all conventional medicine and emergency assistance required. Some also offer very nice birthing suites with birth pools and overnight accommodation for partners. An increasing number of midwives are knowledgeable, if not fully trained and qualified in more natural birthing methods, therapies and remedies for pregnancy. Some people feel that they need the security of a hospital for the birth of their first child but there is an equal chance of a normal birth at home whether it's the first child or not. Another bonus is that midwives are on hand to take care of the baby should mum need to rest.

A hospital, however, may not feel as relaxed as a home environment and there may be a large turnaround of staff which can be quite stressful. A relaxed mum equals a straightforward birth! There may be more chance of medical interventions at a hospital and waiting until staff are available to help mother and baby with things such as bathing after the birth is the norm. In fact you'll have to wait for everything and endure a lack of privacy during visiting hours too! The food is awful and hospitals are too hot and full of ill people. Expectant mums are not ill they are having a baby!

If breastfeeding is preferred, make sure that the hospital has the UNICEF/WHO Baby Friendly Accreditation. This means that their midwives are fully trained in encouraging and supporting breastfeeding. Bear in mind that there may be a wait until a midwife becomes available to help out. If using cloth/reusable nappies is a priority, make sure that the hospital can accommodate this as many don't. Watch out that they don't wash your baby in anything but water too. All too often that squirt of chemical smelly stuff is on the baby's head before you so much as squeak your resistance, despite recommendations that babies be bathed in nothing but water for the first six months of their life. If a water birth is preferred, find out whether birthing is allowed in the pool or whether mums have to get out to birth. Also, find out if both parents are allowed in the pool. Each hospital has its own policy. It's also worth checking the normal birth rate and caesarean section rates of the hospitals in your area which can be found on the Internet. Depending on where you live, try searching on the area, hospital name and the words 'birth statistics'.

Last but not least, many people don't realize that they are entitled to have their baby at a hospital of their choice. They believe that if they are receiving state treatment, they automatically have to go to their closest hospital, but this is not the case. Once you've chosen a hospital make sure they're informed and write the name of the hospital in the birth plan. Be sure of your choice, as any late changes may not be accommodated.

Pros:

- *safety and security of having all medical aid to hand, especially for first time mums or those with complications*
- *some may have private rooms and free use of birth pools*
- *no need to tidy up afterwards*
- *midwifes on hand to look after baby while you catch up on some sleep*
- *help with breastfeeding, bathing and nappy changing.*

Cons:

- *lack of privacy*
- *clinical atmosphere*
- *bad food*
- *high turnover of staff*
- *more impersonal service*
- *hospital superbugs*

- *may not feel as relaxed as a home environment*
- *may be quicker to turn to medical intervention.*

HOME BIRTH

This doesn't really have any major cons apart from the fact that some women prefer the security of a hospital birth. It may take longer to receive emergency assistance and of course there's likely to be some tidying up to do afterwards. In the event of suspected distress, a birth attendant may wish to monitor the baby's heart using an electronic heart monitor which can involve a move to hospital. However, foetal heart monitors can now be rented for home use and it is possible to request that the birth attendant uses a hand held monitor.

A home birth will ensure a familiar and loving environment with all personal possessions to hand. It's private and there is no need to feel self-conscious about screaming or having a sudden urge for a number two (and this is just the partners). At home you'll be attended by a team of community midwives or other chosen birth attendants, all of whom both parents can meet before the birth. The birth environment can be tailored to suit your mood with no restrictions on the use of candles, music or aromas. You can walk around outside and have as many people in attendance as you like. Gas and air will be delivered to your home in advance of the due date so that it's there should it be required and if conventional pain relief becomes a must it can be made available. Should complications develop, hospital is but an ambulance ride away. Breastfeeding should be a natural progression and the midwife or birth attendant will not leave until mother and baby have confidently and contentedly established feeding. Parents can also choose whatever birthing aids and equipment they like and a warm relaxing bath is just a stroll away.

Pros:

- *a relaxed environment tailored to your needs*
- *less chance of medical intervention*

- *one to one assistance without high turnover of staff*
- *a more personal quiet experience*
- *you can have anyone you like present and walk around wherever you want*
- *basic medical help and pain relief available.*

Cons:

- *in the event of complications may take longer to receive emergency treatment*
- *have to pay for use of birth pool if required*
- *you'll have to tidy up.*

DOMINO SCHEME

This is a system which places the mother under the care of the community midwives throughout the pregnancy. They will come to the house whilst the mother is in labour then the family is transferred to hospital when birth is imminent. Mother and baby are discharged around six hours later and post-natal needs are taken care of at home. The benefit of the scheme is that parents get to know their midwives and it's a good compromise between hospital and home. GPs or midwives can advise on which hospitals offer this scheme.

Pros:

- *all the benefits of a hospital birth*
- *back in comfort of own home as soon as possible.*

Cons:

- *all the drawbacks of a hospital birth*
- *the mother has to pack up and go home instead of just relaxing.*

BIRTH CENTRES

These are medically equipped centres for births which are designed to have a homelike atmosphere with space to walk around in whilst in labour, birth pools and/or partner accommodation. They promote more natural methods of birth including active birth and a few of the professionals there will be qualified in some form of natural therapy. Should a mother require it, all modern medical equipment is available including operating theatres in some larger birth centres. State run birth centres may be consultant and/or midwife led. Privately run birth centres are generally midwife led. State birth centres are free but private ones can be expensive although some may offer subsidized places. There are a limited number of birth centres and, therefore, limited places.

Pros:

- ▶ *all the benefits of a hospital*
- ▶ *more relaxed atmosphere than a hospital*
- ▶ *more emphasis on natural or active birth*
- ▶ *many midwives trained in more natural birth methods and complimentary therapies*
- ▶ *private accommodation with provision for partners to stay too.*

Cons:

- ▶ *some must be paid for and are expensive*
- ▶ *places may be limited*
- ▶ *still have to transfer to home at some point.*

Birth assistance

As part of the birth plan, parents may be asked who'll be attending the birth. If you're not asked, make sure you make it clear anyway. Who attends the birth may affect how supported the mother feels and any decisions that are made. Traditionally, birth partners were female members of the family or a respected matron or birth assistant in the community, with a doctor on hand if things didn't go to plan. Nowadays, although we are much better prepared medically we seem to have lost the maternal support part which is vital to both parents.

Whether birthing at home or hospital, consider having a close female relative or friend as a birth partner to help both of you, if a partner will also attend the birth. Ideally this extra person will have had children or be sympathetic and understanding of exactly what kind of birth you'd like. Make sure they are familiar with the birth plan and that they are confident about the task in hand. This means that a partner and birth partner can take it in turns to rest and are both equally capable of communicating wishes to midwives and doctors should they need to. The birth partner should also be someone with whom both parents feel mutually comfortable with.

A PARTNER'S ROLE AT BIRTH

This has changed through the ages. Not so long ago men were considered to be more of a hindrance than a help at childbirth with the whole process being the domain of women. Things began to change in the seventies when men began to be more involved in the birth process and hospitals began to accept their attendance at the birth. There are now some researchers who think that the old fashioned way may well be the best! While sharing the experience is amazing there is a lot to be said for allowing a woman to go through labour with her chosen birth partners with a partner joining in for the birth. A loving partner can be a great help through the birth process but can also become stressed and exhausted when they see the person they love go through a long and painful labour.

It's very much down to personal choice. A partner who is calm and well prepared (through Active Birth classes or otherwise) can help communicate the birth plan to birth attendants, help deal with pain through operating a TENS machine, carry out massage and visualization and can aid general relaxation. It is an experience you will share for the rest of your lives.

They will normally be midwives in the hospital or community midwives who will attend a home birth if this is the preferred choice. As previously discussed, parents can also decide to have a close friend or relative to act as an additional birth partner. However, if you can afford it and feel the need for some back-up you can also employ the services of an independent midwife. An independent midwife has the same skills as a hospital midwife and is also trained in active birth and natural remedies. Another option is a doula. The word 'doula' originates from Greek and means 'woman caregiver of another woman'. A doula is essentially a birth servant to the expectant mother. As well as being employed to be present for the birth she can also be employed both before and after the birth to help you cope with everything from sleepless nights to housework. A doula's focus is the mother and helping her to have as natural and as healthy a birth as possible, but while she will assist the birth alongside a doctor and or midwife she does not actually birth the baby. She is there purely as a trained and knowledgeable support for the mother, a bit like an old fashioned local matron!

You can find a doula or independent midwife by asking other mums, checking with local health professionals or using online forums. Many doulas and independent midwives are part of wider organizations who list their practitioners according to the area they cover. You can find these organizations on the Internet. Personal recommendations are great. And remember that both mother and partner have to feel comfortable with the person you choose, so meet potential birth attendants before making a definite choice and take your time. Whoever you choose to attend the birth, make sure you are completely happy with your choice and that everyone is fully aware of your birth plan.

How to birth

Birthing is a huge subject about which numerous books have been written. Again the most practical green advice one can give is to get informed and just try to do things as naturally as possible whilst making sure that you feel comfortable with the decisions you've made. If this aspect of green parenting really interests you it's a good idea to invest some time in researching the finer details of natural birth. Some books are suggested at the end of this book but it's also a good idea to search the Internet and use your local library.

ACTIVE BIRTH

As mentioned before, this is a method of birthing which puts the mother back in control by allowing her to move around during her labour into positions which are the most comfortable for normal birth. Depending on the stage of labour these could be walking, standing, sitting, kneeling or squatting with the baby usually being born with the mother in an upright position. Gravity helps a baby move down the birth canal to be born. Assuming upright positions helps gravity help nature do its thing! During the process the mother is supported by massage and other forms of natural birthing remedies and is reassured that her body is perfectly able to manage natural birth whilst having the safety net of modern medicine should it be required. Active birth also involves the participation of the birth partners in attendance which is a great way to ensure that a partner is involved and proactive in the birthing process.

WATER BIRTH

This is a birth that takes place in a large warm pool of water called a birthing pool. The actual birth may not take place in the water. This is dependent on the wishes of the individual, the medical situation and hospital policy (if relevant) but many women find the warmth and floating sensation of being in the birthing pool has a calming and pain relieving effect which can help labour progress. Warm water can lower high blood pressure and reduce pain due to a reduction in stress hormones, the loss of the effects of gravity and an increase in the hormones which control relaxation and pain (endorphins). For nine months the baby thrives in the watery environment of the amniotic fluid in the womb. Many parents believe that birthing in water ensures a gentle transition from the womb to a new life on land. One pioneer of water birth is

Michel Odent who first thought of using warm water to ease labour pain. If you would like more information on water birth some of his books are recommended at the back of this book.

As mentioned before, many hospitals have birthing pools, but do check availability and booking procedures beforehand and also the hospital's policy on actually birthing in the pool. Birthing pools may also be hired or bought. Ask your doctor, doula or midwife for more information or check the Internet for a supplier near you. Personal recommendations are best as they offer peace of mind and ensure an efficient service.

HYPNOBIRTHING

You can go to classes which educate women and their partners about how to use simple hypnosis techniques to help the process of labour and birth. Hypnosis is a naturally induced state of relaxation similar to the state we slip in and out of during a normal day as we watch television and go about routine tasks. The philosophy of hypnobirthing is that childbirth does not need to be painful and through managing the expectation and fear of pain through hypnosis it can be dealt with more easily. Hypnobirthing claims to be able to shorten labour, reduce pain and hence the need for medication resulting in healthier newborns and new mums!

While the best choices are classes with a live teacher with whom you can interact, the cost of these classes may put some people off. Subsidized classes are available but could be hard to find. There are many childbirth education courses offered on DVD, book format and even online.

Pain relief during labour and birth

We have already mentioned various forms of natural pain relief for pregnancy and birth. However, an array of pain relief and other drugs designed to aid labour and birth will be offered. Because all drugs administered to the mother will be transferred to the baby it is important to know what these drugs are, what they are used for and their possible side effects. It is the parents' right to decide what kind of medicines are used for mother and child and to insist on a more natural alternative if it's available. Remember to include these preferences in the birth plan too. In order to help you become familiar with all the technical medical jargon and to help you make an informed choice, the various options are listed below. Remember that if you're unsure about anything ask your doctor, midwife or health professional until you fully understand. It's your choice!

VALIUM

This is used for pain management and to help the mother deal with stress. It may cause amnesia to the mother and can be passed rapidly to the baby.

PETHIDINE

This is also used for pain relief. It can affect the breathing response and the sucking reflex of the baby which may hinder breastfeeding. It can cause nausea and drowsiness in the mother but can help dilation if given in small doses. If given in the late stages of labour it can remain in the baby's system for a few days. Mother to baby bonding may be disturbed if both are still drowsy at first contact.

BUPIVACAINE

This is used for epidurals which give pain relief from the waist down without loss of consciousness. It is extremely useful for caesarean sections as the mother can remain awake during the operation which allows her to bond with her baby when it's born. However, due to the fact that an epidural reduces the function of the uterus and bladder, a catheter needs to be fitted and when it is used for pain relief during the last stages of labour the weakened uterus may result in the need for a forceps delivery. The mother may also not be able to push due to lack of sensation. After-effects such as headaches can last up to a week for some women. It can lower the blood pressure of the mother and thus limit the amount of oxygen available to the baby as this drug enters the baby's bloodstream in minutes. The effects on the baby are less than pethidine, but can cause the baby to be drowsy or nervy.

GAS AND OXYGEN (ETENOX)

These do enter the baby's bloodstream but the effects are inconclusive. Taken in large amounts it can make the mother feel 'trippy'. It may help some women cope with the final stages of labour but others report that it made them feel confused and delayed the desire to push.

TRILENE

This can make mother and baby drowsy and sleepy.

SYNTOCIN OR OXYTOCIN DRIP

This is used to stimulate contractions and accelerate labour. It can cause the baby to become distressed as the contractions can be so strong that they interrupt blood flow to the placenta. Due to stronger contractions there may be the need for pain relief drugs as the mother could find it difficult to cope. A failed induction may result in a caesarean section.

SYNOMETRINE

This is an intramuscular injection routinely used to induce the final stage of labour. It may make mother feel nauseous and require that the cord is clamped immediately removing the choice for the cord to be cut only when it has stopped functioning, after the baby's breathing is fully established.

Please remember that if there are serious complications medication can provide a valuable safety net. This can be combined with natural methods of pain relief to aid both mother and child. However the routine use of medication is unnecessary and can have harmful effects on mother and child.

NATURAL PAIN RELIEF

There are numerous different methods of natural pain relief for labour, i.e. methods that do not involve the use of conventional medication or medical procedures. Try combining one or more of the options detailed below.

TENS machine
This is a battery operated or electrically operated machine which emits electrical pulses via electrodes to the areas of pain. They can be hired from some hospitals and shops or bought from most mainstream pharmacies. The pain relief works by causing the muscles to tense and relax when stimulated by the electric current. It's a strange sensation at first but some women find that a TENS machine is useful during early stages of labour.

Birthing ball
This is a large air-filled ball (a bit like an adult sized space hopper!) which can also be used for pilates and other forms of exercise. It can be used during labour to sit in an upright position without putting too much pressure on the perineal area. They are also useful for leaning on, draping over to find a good birthing position and for sitting on and rolling the hips to relieve pain.

Bathing or showering
A bath or shower in warm water is the original natural pain reliever. Whilst a plain old bath is absolutely fine check your local area for birthing specialists that will hire out pools large enough for both parents to get into. Showers can help too and it's a good idea to find a low stable stool that can be placed under the shower so that you don't have to stand the whole time.

Effleurage
This is a light rhythmic stroking of the abdomen back or thighs. It's better done on bare skin with the tips of the fingers by a birth partner. A little cornstarch on the fingers ensures a silky smooth touch. Ask a midwife or doula for more information or look it up on the Internet or in the local library.

Essential oils

These can be useful during pregnancy. If there is a particular aroma that evokes feelings of calmness and serenity try to stock up and have a good supply at hand. They can be burned in a diffuser, added to bathwater, dabbed onto cloth and kept nearby or onto a damp facecloth for the forehead. Always check with a book or practitioner first as some are not suitable during pregnancy. Oils which should definitely be avoided during pregnancy are birch, wintergreen, wormwood, cotton lavender and rue. Some of these are prohibited and not generally available anyway. A slight caution exists for the use of clary sage early on in the pregnancy if you are at a high risk of miscarriage.

Massage

This will be much appreciated at the end of pregnancy. The lower back and inner thighs will really benefit. Don't be afraid to experiment though. Labouring mothers can try standing with their back to a wall holding a tennis ball against the lower back and moving the ball around to relieve local back pain.

Labour positions

Try standing upright or going down on all fours during labour. Changing positions often may help relieve discomfort. Active birth books or classes will help understanding about these postures and how a birth partner can help support the mother in the postures. It's good to become familiar with different postures so that you can quickly find out which ones might work best during labour.

Exercise

Walking, yoga and a bit of light housework during the early onset of labour can relieve the sensation of pain and help ensure that the labour progresses as well as providing a bit of distraction.

Hot and cold compresses

These are useful to relieve pain not only in the small of the back, neck and shoulders but also on the perineum. Hot water bottles or cherry stone bags are useful.

Breathing techniques
These are taught by most childbirth classes both privately and through standard ante-natal classes held at your hospital. They are also taught at yoga classes. Regulated breathing helps mothers to remain calm and cope with pain.

Hypnosis and visualization
This may be taught at childbirth education classes or, cost permitting, consider a private hypnotherapist who can give hypnotic suggestion training which helps patients react to pain in a different way, so that it doesn't hurt so much. Visualizing labour can help mothers prepare for birth. Imagining each stage and the ease with which the baby will move down the birth canal and slide out into the world helps some women to manage their pain.

Acupuncture
Acupuncture is not only good for pain relief during the birth but also for helping to move the baby's position in the womb. It is extremely effective for pain relief with no side effect for mother or baby. In China, acupuncture is used instead of anaesthetic epidural during caesarean sections! If you're interested in acupuncture for labour and birth try to find a registered practitioner who is willing to attend the birth.

Acupressure
This involves applying pressure to known pressure points in the body which in turn relieve symptoms of pain in other parts of the body. Birth partners can learn these techniques ahead of time to use during labour.

Bach flower remedies
Try these for soothing and calming during childbirth. Rescue Remedy is especially good for mother and birth partner. Each flower essence is designed to relieve a specific emotion or fear and can be bought in most good chemist and natural health stores. There are also many good books available on the subject.

Homeopathy
Use this throughout pregnancy, labour and beyond. Arnica is particularly useful. Arm yourself with a pregnancy homeopathy kit (available at most natural health stores) and do some swotting up on what and how much to take during the different phases of labour. Better still, try to enlist the help of a midwife or doula who has homeopathic training.

Music
Some women find this soothing and distracting while others prefer silence. Studies have shown that music can help with pain relief so make sure the chosen hospital or birth centre allows the playing of music if you think this might work for you.

If you'd like more information about the therapies mentioned above, they are covered in Chapter 7 in more detail. Research has shown that fear and a lack of confidence about the birthing process affects a woman's response to and ability to deal with pain which is why preparation for the birth experience is a valuable investment. Further study has shown that pain need not be completely eliminated to give a more fulfilling birth experience and that the pain of childbirth is different to the pain of injury because it has a purpose and end result. It's really important for labouring mothers to keep the final product firmly in mind!

Caesarean sections

This is a surgical procedure which involves making a small horizontal incision just above the pubic bone and removing the baby from the uterus through this incision. Most sections are carried out under epidural anaesethic which means that the mother is numbed from the waist down but is fully awake during the procedure. It is now very unlikely that anything goes wrong during a caesarean section and when a vaginal birth is impossible caesarean sections are a marvel of modern medicine. Caesarean sections should only be used in the case of an emergency but in practice they are often used before the possibility of a vaginal birth has been completely ruled out. There may be a variety of reasons for this such as convenience, routine, lack of confidence and, unbelievably, fashion. This applies not only to the medical establishment but also to mothers. In America, one in four babies is born by caesarean section!

Becoming aware of what a caesarean section is, preparing for birth, understanding the pregnant body and how the medical profession approach birth will help avoid an unnecessary caesarean section. A vaginal birth allows all the natural physical and emotional reactions to take place between mother and baby such as breathing, alertness, eye to eye contact and bonding. Mums and babies who are groggy due to anaesthetic drugs may find it more tricky to establish breastfeeding and an abdominal incision can lead to infection and may affect future pregnancies. Unnecessary caesarean sections may also cause psychological stress to the mother and result in subsequent post-natal depression. It is extremely important therefore, to make any feelings about caesarean sections clear in the birth plan. However, mothers who have no option about whether or not to have a caesarean section are not jeopardizing bonding with their children as there are lots of ways to naturally optimize this when a vaginal birth has not been possible.

REASONS FOR EMERGENCY CAESAREANS

The following are emergency situations where a caesarean section may be necessary, depending on circumstances.

Placentia previa
The placenta grows partially or completely over the cervical opening. It is sometimes possible to have a vaginal delivery if the placenta is only partially covering the opening, otherwise a section is always required. However, early diagnosis of this condition should be monitored as it can correct itself during the course of a pregnancy.

Prolapsed umbilical cord
The umbilical cord comes out of the cervix before the baby does. This can cut off the baby's oxygen supply and usually requires an emergency caesarean section.

Transverse lie
The baby is in a sideways position in the mother's belly. Birth attendants can try to change the position of a baby lying in this position. However, if these attempts are not successful a caesarean section is necessary.

Decision to end pregnancy early
This may happen if the baby has a medical condition which may be better treated and monitored outside the womb.

Severe pre-eclampsia
The blood pressure rises to dangerously high levels. Drugs may help to treat this and a vaginal birth may be possible but if not, a caesarean section before due date may be recommended but each case needs to be judged on its own merits.

Diabetes
This can be monitored during pregnancy and controlled through diet but in instances where it is uncontrollable a caesarean section may be recommended.

Caesarean sections may be unnecessary in the following circumstances.

Failure to progress
When labour is going on for a long time without progressing, it's important that you are satisfied that this will result in a valid health risk. It may just be that it's taking too long to be accommodated by the medical staff.

Foetal distress
When the baby is becoming stressed during the delivery, this can be detected by the presence of meconium, which is the unborn

baby's poo, or picked up by a foetal monitor. Slight signs of stress may not necessarily require surgery and may just mean that the mother needs to eat or rest. Different health professionals seem to have different ideas about when intervention is necessary and a fear of legal repercussions may lead them to play it safe and resort to surgery.

Breech position
The baby comes out legs or buttocks first instead of head first. This does not automatically mean that a caesarean section is required but many health professionals automatically recommend this. There are several natural ways of dealing with a breach birth and some midwives may even be specially trained in birthing babies in the breach position. Alternatively there are exercises mothers can do at home to help a breech baby to turn such as the breech tilt. Walking for an hour a day may also encourage the baby to turn. Homeopathy (one single dose of 10m pulsatilla) and an acupuncture treatment called moksha may also be used. Acupuncture seems to be particularly successful. A doctor or midwife may also attempt to externally turn the baby using manipulation of the mother's abdomen.

Twins
Surgical delivery may be necessary if one is distressed, one is underweight or there are health issues. Because of this the vaginal delivery of twins seems to be becoming a bit of a lost art. If you're determined to birth twins naturally try to find an understanding and skilled midwife or hire the services of a doula or independent midwife.

Cephalopelvic disproportion
The baby's head is too large to pass through the pelvis. Although health professionals may schedule in a caesarean section for a suspected case, the condition is rare and can only be accurately determined at the time of labour so it's worth trying for a natural birth first with the back-up of a section if required. The condition is quite different from just having a large baby, which many petite women have successfully birthed.

Health problems in the mother
Conditions such as diabetes and hypertension don't necessarily require a section but may be recommended just to be on the safe side.

Previous caesarean section
Refer to the next section on vaginal births after a caesarean section.

Convenience
This should never be a valid reason for a surgical birth, for either the mother or the health professional involved. Caesarean sections are major surgery and carry with them all the usual potential complications and discomforts of surgery and also deny the mother and child of all the benefits of labour and natural birth.

VAGINAL BIRTH AFTER A CAESAREAN SECTION (VBAC)

VBAC is just as safe as repeated surgery, provided there are no major complications, and allows the mother and baby to have a trauma free birth experience and overall feeling of being in control. Some health professionals recommend against trying for a vaginal birth after a caesarean section, but research has shown that going into labour, even if it does end in a section, is beneficial to the baby's alertness and respiratory system so it's worth giving it a try. The main safety concern of VBAC is the risk of uterine rupture (when the uterus slowly tears). However, this is relatively rare and is highly unlikely to result in a life threatening situation as it is accompanied by easily recognizable symptoms and action can be taken immediately. Uterine rupture sounds worse than it is and can happen to any woman in any pregnancy, not only those who've had a section.

The only decisive indications that a woman should not attempt a VBAC are conditions such as placenta previa and abruption placenta, a baby who is clearly distressed, or cephalopelvic disproportion, when the baby's head is too big to fit through the birth canal.

The success of VBAC is influenced by environment, birth attendants, the health of the mother and baby and how informed the mother and her birth attendants are. The success rates of VBAC vary from country to country and from hospital to hospital. If you do decide to go for a VBAC research the facility and practitioners you want to use. Try to use a practitioner with a high success rate for VBAC (about 70 per cent), who is understanding, totally supportive of your choice and will be able to support you through the labour.

If you decide to go for a hospital birth make sure you are comfortable with the hospital and when you go for your tour of the hospital speak to the staff and check out their attitude toward VBAC. If you don't feel the staff are enthusiastic try another hospital or birth centre or aim to birth at home with the support of an independent midwife or doula. VBAC is a prime example of how woman to woman support can aid a smooth delivery. Learn all you can about VBAC and consider contacting a support network such as the National Childbirth Trust, International Caesarean Action Network, The Association of Radical Midwives or the Association for Improvement in the Maternity Services.

CUTTING THE CORD

After the birth of your baby a rush of emotions will cause a hormonal reaction to begin contractions which will expel the placenta from the uterus. Breastfeeding can aid this natural process. As this happens your baby will slowly have begun to breathe independently. When a baby is breathing completely independently the umbilical cord stops pulsating. It becomes floppy and clamps itself. It is at this point that it's safe to cut the cord or you can wait until the placenta is delivered too. Many parents like to request that they are allowed to cut the cord. This can be a very touching experience for your partner. Many hospitals use Syntometrine (as described earlier) to induce the contractions that expel the placenta. It is your right to request that this is not used unless completely necessary. Either way, make sure you include this in your birth plan.

How to make the transition to parenthood easier

No matter where you intend to birth, it's a good idea to start getting yourself prepared a month or so before the end of your pregnancy so you don't have to worry about it later. Cook and freeze some food ahead of time. Ask friends and family to cook, clean and shop to help out rather than them buying baby gifts. Consider using paper plates, and cups (try to get ones made of recycled paper if possible) to cut down on any cleaning up that needs to be done. Prepare birth announcements and thank you cards if you intend to give these out. If you have a bit of spare cash consider employing a cleaner for the first few weeks to help you out. Have some nice clean sheets and treat yourself to a new nightgown after the birth.

Here are two handy lists of things you'll need to take with you to the hospital or have at home in preparation for a home birth. These are only a guide, so just amend them to suit your needs.

Hospital list

▶ *Nightwear × 2 (specially adapted nursing ones if you prefer)*
▶ *Slippers or flip flops*
▶ *Hot water bottle or heat pads and ice packs*
▶ *Massage oil and massage devices such as a tennis ball*
▶ *Essential oils such as lavender*
▶ *Nourishing snacks such as bananas and cereal bars for both you and your partner*
▶ *Herbal teas*
▶ *Swimsuit for your partner should you both want to use the birth pool*
▶ *Music and CD player*
▶ *Candles and matches*
▶ *Large sanitary towels (reusable ones if desired)*
▶ *Witch hazel or other soothing cream for perineal area*
▶ *A camera or video camera*
▶ *Phone numbers of friends and family you'd like to contact after the birth*

- *Nursing bra and nursing pads (washable if desired)*
- *Reusable nappies or eco-disposables and wraps (at least 5)*
- *Waterproof bags for taking home soiled nappies (if in hospital)*
- *Baby clothes that have been washed and that you've kept in your bed before the birth so that your baby recognizes your smell*
- *Swaddling blanket if required*
- *Really big comfy pants*
- *Baby car seat*
- *Lip balm*
- *Pampering cosmetics and hair accessories*
- *Make sure the hospital can provide a TENS machine and/or birthing ball and if it can't, take your own*
- *Anything that you find inspirational!*

Home list
- *Curtains or blinds to darken room*
- *Dimmers on lights or candles and lamps*
- *Beanbags or large cushions*
- *A comfortable stool or birth ball for squatting on*
- *A comfortable chair*
- *Hand held heart monitor*
- *TENS machine*
- *Essential oils*
- *Homeopathy birth kit*
- *Kettle*
- *Snacks and juices for mother and birth assistants*
- *Herbal teas*
- *CD player*
- *Towels and wash cloths*
- *Old newspapers*
- *Big bowl to catch the placenta*
- *Antiseptic soap*
- *Alcohol rub*
- *A work area near your birthing place for your birth attendant*
- *A place for your birth attendants to rest*
- *Snacks and refreshments for all*
- *Plastic sheets for bed (an old shower curtain will do).*

Green parent guide to birth

🌿 Try to stay at home for as long as possible during labour and avoid pain relief drugs as much as possible. Try not to lie down to give birth and keep moving around during labour as much as possible.

🌿🌿 Try a domino birth and prepare yourself for the birth using perineal massage and the other suggestions mentioned. Try to find a midwife who is trained in at least one complimentary therapy and is sympathetic to your requirements. Use natural pain relief during the birth and birth as actively as possible.

🌿🌿🌿 Aim for a holistic birth by preparing your mind and body with yoga, active birth classes, massage, nutrition and visualization. Birth at home with the help of a Doula and as little medical intervention as possible. Hire a birth pool and use the Active Birth method. Maximize your birth environment with candles, music and aromatherapy oils. Make sure your birth partner is knowledgeable about your chosen natural pain relief methods. Aim to deliver the placenta naturally without the aid of drugs and only allow a person of your choice to clamp the cord when it has stopped pulsating.

3

After the birth

In this chapter you will learn:
- *how to maximize natural bonding with your baby*
- *how to deal with sleeping and eating patterns*
- *about well-being after the birth.*

The period after childbirth is a special and important time for parents, close friends and family to welcome a new baby. Many parents talk about being in a bubble of love and closeness where everything has an unreal quality. Others talk about being unsure and confused. No matter how it is for your new family make sure you allow time to be a new family.

The babymoon

Just like a marriage, many cultures around the world believe that a new family needs time to bond. In India, Ayurvedic belief dictates that mother and baby are not disturbed and remain in solitude for twenty two days allowing them time to bond, whilst in other countries mother and child are celebrated by friends and family with a grand feast when the period of confinement ends. Unfortunately our culture seems to have lost much of its reverence for the purity and wonder of childbirth. Often it's not financially practical to have too much time off work, and with so many families living far away from their close relatives, parents often find themselves without a support network that would allow them to take time out with a new child. Whatever your personal situation, try to allow at least two weeks for you and your family to enjoy and learn about each other with as few visitors as possible. Ask friends and family to help out with things like getting the shopping. If you can afford one, make sure a post-natal doula helps out around the house allowing you family bonding time together.

Bonding

Mothers may bond instantly with their newborn child or it may take a few weeks. There is no norm for this but time out from your normal routine and limiting visitors can definitely aid mother and child bonding.

Partners are also an important part of the bonding process. Not only can they bond by helping with the care of the baby but they will also bond with the mother as a family unit by helping and caring for her. Mothers, especially if breastfeeding, will share a strong physiological bond with their baby, but in most cultures mothers are not the sole carers of a child and parenting works extremely well if the care is shared, and parents or carers trust and support each other.

A partner may bond and love their baby in a different way to the mother. As well as a strong protective instinct they may want to become immediately involved in the practical care of the baby. Partners shouldn't hesitate to hold the baby close, including skin to skin contact and all the other techniques described in this chapter. A partner's smell and heartbeat will become familiar to the baby and confidence will build. Babies don't care whether tasks are carried out perfectly, they just need tender care.

Bonding can be aided in several ways not only by skin to skin contact, but also by singing and talking to your baby, baby wearing, baby massage, feeding on demand and bed sharing. These techniques when used in combination are often referred to as attachment parenting.

ATTACHMENT PARENTING

This was a term coined ten years ago to describe a parenting technique that is aware of and responsive to the needs of a child during the attachment period (the first 3–5 years of life). Underpinning this method of parenting is the importance of a responsive, nurturing and continually present carer. Disruptions in this early bond are believed to lead to an adulthood prone to depression, anxiety and relationship problems. According to various experts on the subject, attachment parenting contains the following components.

Bed sharing or co-sleeping

Some people recommend that newborn babies sleep with their parents in the family bed. There are several benefits to this including ease of breastfeeding and tuning into your baby's needs. Babies who co-sleep tend to sleep better and parental sleep patterns fall in synchronization with the baby's, making it easier to cope during the day. Closeness of body heat helps regulate baby's body temperature and also provides an opportunity for skin to skin contact and bonding. This helps the baby's emotional development.

Parents benefit by sharing quality time with their child, especially if they work during the day. Less crying and the fact that a parent doesn't need to wake fully to breastfeed means a more restful night for mum and dad! One of the biggest benefits however is the prevention of cot death or SIDS (Sudden Infant Death Syndrome). The Foundation for the Study of Infant Deaths (FSID) recommends that babies sleep in their parent's room for at least the first six months. Research has shown that this can significantly reduce the incidence of SIDS because parents are more aware of their baby's activity and breathing patterns. When co-sleeping, the parents breathing rhythm actually reminds the baby to breathe, even in sleep. In cultures where sleeping with babies is the norm, SIDS is virtually unknown!

Co-sleeping can take the form of actually sleeping with your baby in your bed, having your baby in a cot right next to your bed with the side removed as a kind of extension of your own bed or merely having the cot in your room. Whichever option you go for, or a combination of each to suit your needs, having baby in the same room as you will have benefits for both parents and child. Although a period of six months plus is recommended, you may find that you become so in tune with your baby's needs that you'll recognize her prompts when she's ready to move on to having her own sleeping arrangements.

Co-sleeping will not make baby more dependent on you and if you naturally and gradually introduce independence when both parents and baby are ready, the transition to her own room should be smooth. Many parents worry about accidentally smothering their child when co-sleeping, but mothers tend to have a constant awareness of their baby, even whilst sleeping, and babies have a very effective early warning system.

Insight

Please note, however, parents should never co-sleep with their baby if they've been drinking alcohol, smoking or taking recreational drugs, because this greatly increases the risk of infant death.

Make sure the bed is big enough to fit everyone in comfortably and the mattress is fairly firm. Babies should be positioned so that they will not fall out of the bed and will not be smothered by pillows or bedding. Make sure that everyone, including baby, are dressed in light bed clothes and aren't too warm.

The Department of Health recommends that babies sleep in a cot or crib in their parents' room for the first six months. The UNICEF Baby Friendly Initiative, however, do not support blanket recommendations against bed sharing in the early weeks. The Royal College of Midwives recommends that parents should be made aware of all the issues involved with co-sleeping so that they can make their own decisions. The controversy over the safety of co-sleeping makes it doubly important for you as a parent to arm yourself with as much information as possible and make an informed decision.

Babies should sleep on their backs until they are at least six months old. Your baby will probably prompt you by turning over when ready to adopt a different sleeping position. Use sheets or blankets instead of a duvet and never fall asleep with your baby lying on you. Parents should sleep with their baby between them rather then at the edge of the bed or near a wall.

Baby wearing

This simply means using a sling, front carrier or backpack to carry baby around for the first few months of life, enabling you to get on with your everyday tasks. Traditional cultures all over the world carry babies using cloth sarongs, blankets or baby carriers. Contrary to some modern beliefs, a baby who is carried a lot will not become clingy or demanding but secure and content.

Baby wearing helps build intimate bonds, making baby feel safe and secure. It also helps avoid post-natal depression in mothers. Being carried a lot helps the baby develop muscle tone and posture, stimulates brain development and learning, is good for a baby's digestion and can limit colic and reflux as well as allowing quick and easy feeding.

Slings and carriers are now available in a variety of shapes, sizes, colours and styles. Babies can be carried in a variety of positions according to age. For example, side slings are especially good for newborns as they replicate the foetal position in the womb and allow even pressure along the length of the baby's spine. Front carriers allow the baby to face inward and then, as baby gets older, outward. Backpacks can be used once your baby can sit unsupported.

Many health professionals offer good advice on slings to suit your individual needs and websites and shops now offer individual specialist advice too. It's worth attending baby sales and looking at swap and sell Internet sites for really good, used slings at a reasonable price.

Skin to skin contact

Parents and babies bond when familiar with each others' smell and touch. Skin to skin contact stimulates the production of colostrum, the important nutrient and antibody-rich first breast milk. Ideal opportunities for skin to skin contact are during feeding, sleeping and cuddling.

Bathing with baby is another great way to achieve skin to skin contact but also makes getting clean fun and is fantastic preparation for swimming. Make sure the bathroom is warm and the bath water no hotter than 29°C. Prepare the bath with a non-slip bath mat and make sure you have towels ready for baby when you get out. It's a good idea to have someone around who can help you get in and out of the bath with your baby, and remember there's no need for soap or bubbles for a newborn. A touch of olive oil works wonders if you really need to give your baby a good clean. It can also be very relaxing to feed your baby whilst in the bath.

Baby massage
This has been practiced in different cultures for centuries. Touch and movement are amongst the first senses to develop in the womb, so massage really helps a newborn to feel comfortable in its new external environment and to build close intimate bonds with its parents. Baby massage also helps soothe and relax, encourages good posture and optimal development, promotes muscle co-ordination and flexible joints, improves breathing, stimulates digestion and the immune system, aids sleep, relieves pain and many common ailments, as well as providing an opportunity for play.

Prepare for massage by ensuring that the environment is warm and calm and that your baby has something soft to lie on. Choose a comfortable sitting position or massage your baby on the changing table. The best time for massage is when baby is awake and playful or immediately after a bath. Never massage when a baby is hungry or immediately after a feed. Try to end each massage session with a cuddle and a feed. If you massage at regular times each day he will come to anticipate and look forward to this routine.

Massage newborn babies through their clothing at first. Hold your baby close and use gentle stroking or circular movements.

Ten minutes should be plenty at first. Watch your baby for signs that you have done enough and stop immediately if he starts crying.

As your baby gets older and becomes used to lying comfortably whilst undressed, you can massage for a little longer (no more than 20 minutes or until your baby shows signs of boredom) and directly on the skin. Use plain organic sunflower or grape seed oil, making sure you heat the oil in your hands before application. Work slowly and rhythmically over your baby's skin, replenishing the oil frequently and using gentle but steady strokes. As your baby gets older you may want to introduce aromatherapy baby massage oil. For more information on baby massage ask your midwife, doula or health visitor for local classes. There are also many books on the subject as well as lots of valuable information on the Internet.

Feed on demand
Mothers can feed their baby breast milk whenever they need it. If babies are held close to their mother at all times, their needs are more quickly attended to and they tend to cry less. You can find out more about feeding on demand in Chapter 4.

Separation
Avoiding being separated from your baby in its first year of life is a basic element of attachment parenting. For the first year of its life, a baby has no concept that the parent is coming back and generally suffers from distress when separated. For this reason it is believed that it's very important for babies to know that their main caregiver is always around and will continue to be so. Don't worry if your lifestyle means that you cannot fully embrace this parenting method, but do be aware of the importance of contact at this time.

Relying on instinct
Making decisions about what is best for your baby should come naturally if you follow an attachment parenting approach. Research has shown that the hormonal chemistry of birth may

unlock a dormant but instinctual and natural maternal intelligence. Parents must learn to trust this intelligence, and as time goes on they'll become more adept at interpreting and anticipating their baby's needs.

Responding quickly to a baby's cries
This can help parents to distinguish the different types of cries which signify various needs, such as food, comfort, and nappy changes. It is widely believed that babies have a language all of their own, made up of various crying sounds for different needs.

Each of the techniques above can be used separately or in combination according to individual parent's needs. It's also important to recognize that while this method can aid child development and help to nurture well-adjusted happy babies, parents should take time for themselves too. Just as we have forgotten how to take time out and appreciate childbirth and babies and all the natural processes that can go along with it, in our modern, often indulgent western lifestyle, we can have a tendency to overdo things, becoming zealots to our green parenting conversions. This is unnecessary, as in traditional societies, which have inspired the theory of attachment parenting, putting your own life on hold just wouldn't be an option. Try to strike a balance.

Feeding and sleeping patterns

You are bound to be asked by well-meaning admirers if your baby is sleeping through the night yet. If this isn't happening and you're exhausted you may be tempted to let rip. Don't worry, every baby is different and night-time sleep will come. Babies wake when making the transition between different sleep states. This is nature's way of keeping them healthy and well fed. Newborns can't distinguish between day and night and their body rhythms are different to those of adults and children. They wake when they're hungry and sleep when they're full. Periods of sleep may last anywhere between 20 minutes and five hours. Every child is different, but on average a newborn will spend about 60 per cent of their time asleep.

At about six to eight weeks babies begin to sleep more during the night than in the day and their overall sleep time decreases. Some babies can sleep for up to eight hours at a time but this is pretty unusual. Very few babies sleep for more than four hours at a time until they are about four months old. Most babies will have two fairly predictable nap times in the morning and afternoon. Older babies will have one nap in the afternoon which will naturally stop as they get older. Try to encourage night time sleeping in an older baby by keeping him stimulated and active during the day, but if this results in irritation and distress he may not be ready to let go of that daytime nap. As he gets older, sleep patterns will regulate and he will have a longer, more wakeful period during the day.

By the age of six months some babies will be content with three main feeds per day, plus an early morning and late night feed so that parents can get a good stretch of uninterrupted sleep during the night. Sleeping through the night is very likely to consist of a five hour stretch. However, many babies still wake regularly during the night at 12 months old.

If you would like more information on this subject, try *Andrea Grace's Gentle Sleep Solutions* in this series of books. It's a very parent-friendly, objective guide to helping your baby overcome sleep problems.

SLEEP TRAINING

Introducing a regular daytime and evening routine will ensure a more parent-friendly sleep pattern. Make bedtime a special time of day, allowing lots of time to be with your baby. From about four months old babies can be gently taught to fall asleep by themselves without feeding. Once fed, bathed, changed and soothed until relaxed and drowsy, it is best to stay in the room until he falls asleep. If he wakes again resist the temptation to pick up.

Try soothing by rubbing his back or simply laying a hand on him and talking or singing quietly. This approach teaches babies to fall sleep by themselves rather than at the breast or bottle. This may not suit the temperament of every baby so if yours doesn't respond after a few weeks experiment with another method or try again later.

To ensure that everyone gets as much restful sleep as possible, don't delay a feed or replace milk with water or juice if your baby wakes in the night. This will only make him grumpy and unwilling to get back to sleep. A good way to ensure a little extra sleep is to wake him in the late evening for a good feed and a nappy change. This routine may result in four to six hours of uninterrupted sleep and if he does wake, responding quickly will help sleep to come quickly. Regular feeding during the day may also aid night-time sleep.

There has been quite a lot of controversy over certain sleep training methods which are geared towards getting a baby to sleep through the night as soon as possible, in order to fit in with the busy routines and the lifestyle pressures of its parents. These methods generally involve systematically ignoring the baby's cries, withholding night feeds and letting the baby cry until they fall asleep again through exhaustion. For this to work the baby has to sleep alone. A gentler approach can be used, only letting the baby cry for a few minutes at first and gradually increasing the time until he learns this new routine.

Critics of such methods believe this goes against a baby's natural physiology and are concerned it causes the mother's milk production to decrease due to missed night-time breastfeeds. They believe that a baby fed less than it needs may not experience optimal development and a few babies may even be at risk from dehydration. Another criticism is that it causes premature separation between mother and baby.

We can't ask a baby how it feels about being left alone in a room to cry, but it is clear that a baby sleeping in the same room as its parents and being fed at regular intervals during the night will have its needs met. Parents need to consider whether they believe sleep training affects a baby emotionally and if they think it's right for their baby. Do plenty of research on the effects of such sleep training methods and the different ones available before making any decisions.

SLEEP PROBLEMS

Although it is natural for a baby to wake fairly frequently, you may notice times when your baby wakes more often than normal or has difficulty getting to sleep, becoming quite fretful.

There could be several reasons for this. Your baby may be going through a growth spurt, be teething, uncomfortable with its sleeping position or bedding, have colic or some other childhood ailment. Disruption to usual routines or any kind of emotional upset within the family may also cause fretfulness during the night.

For natural remedies to the above common childhood ailments see Chapter 4. If your baby seems upset with its sleeping position, speak to your health professional before changing the position. If there seems to be no cause for your baby's crying consult your doctor and a cranial-sacral therapist. Often, undetected trauma to the skull and spine that occurred during the birth can cause a baby to be fretful. Cranial-sacral therapy has been shown to have results with crying babies in less than 4 treatments. Co-sleeping may help, as well as suckling your baby to sleep. An extended period of crying and trying to settle an upset child can take its toll on parents and there are organizations such as Cry-sis which offer information and counselling. Details can be found at the end of this book.

NATURAL METHODS TO AID SLEEP

As well as the previous suggestions you may want to try:

▶ *making sure your baby sleeps in a darkened room*
▶ *carrying your baby in a sling in the evening and putting her down when asleep*
▶ *lying down with your baby until he drifts off and have a rest yourself but don't fall asleep with your baby on top of you*

- *household sounds, soothing music, lullabies and special recordings of white noise*
- *steady movement such as swaying, rocking and bobbing, wheeling around in a pram or even a ride in the car if you're really desperate*
- *laying your warm hands on your baby's back or head to provide comfort or gently patting or stroking whilst singing to her*
- *finding your baby's comfort spot, often the nape of the neck or forehead, and stroking gently*
- *burning aromatherapy oils in the room before bedtime (check which oils are appropriate with a reputable reference book or practitioner), remembering to put any candles out before you leave the room.*

More information and advice regarding helping your baby to sleep soundly can be found in *Andrea Grace's Gentle Sleep Solutions* (Hodder Education).

Recovering after birth

A woman's body has gone through some incredible physical changes and it will take time to return to its pre-pregnancy state. Throughout the first year of a baby's life it's important for both parents, but especially the main carer, to rest when possible and take time out. It takes approximately six months for the body to recover completely after the birth of a baby. This recovery can be supported by nourishing, healthy food such as miso soup, a traditional Japanese dish combining fermented soya beans and cultured grain. Buy it at your local health food store. Plenty of water and exercise such as yoga, swimming, pilates, walking and moderate gym exercise also aids recovery.

BLEEDING

This can last for up to six weeks after the birth as the uterus sheds the heavy lining it built up during pregnancy. Women should use menstrual pads, not tampons during this time. If using disposables, try to buy unbleached ones from your local health food shop or online. If you want to be really green, buy reusable pads, available from specialist suppliers. Mothers should avoid strenuous activities including excessive exercise and inverted yoga postures until bleeding has stopped as this can cause bleeding to start again and even, in extreme cases, haemorrhage. Eat plenty of iron rich foods to accommodate blood loss including red meat, red beans, lentils, kale, broccoli, raisins, figs, apricots and cherries.

PERINEAL PAIN

This can occur whether or not there was an episiotomy or tear. Some women may experience a stinging sensation, especially when going for a wee. Here are a few tips to aid recovery and make life a little easier for the perineum:

▶ *Take the pressure off the area by using a half moon shaped pillow to sit on (a breastfeeding cushion can double up for this use as well as being an aid to support your baby when he begins to sit up).*
▶ *Instead of using toilet paper try rinsing with water and patting dry with a soft cloth after using the toilet.*
▶ *Prepare a soothing sitz bath with warm hip deep water, three drops of lavender and two drops of cyprus essential oils.*
▶ *Keep some witch hazel or aloe vera gel (or a mixture of both) in the fridge and apply to the perineal area as often as needed.*
▶ *Dilute a few drops of tea tree oil with a 1/2 teaspoon of almond oil and apply to the perineal area, then hold a cloth soaked with warm water to the area to help reduce redness and swelling.*
▶ *Do pelvic floor exercises, starting off with three a day and building up gradually.*

Energy levels will return to normal after about six weeks but new mothers should try to get as much rest as possible in the first few weeks. When baby sleeps, you sleep!

Exercising after birth can begin a few days after birth with pelvic floor exercises, gentle leg lifts and short walks. After three to four weeks it's safe to do gentle stretching exercises, with longer walks, moderate yoga and or light aerobic activity. After three months mums can exercise regularly and by six months most mums should be able to exercise as usual.

MENTAL HEALTH AND THE BABY BLUES

After the babymoon, the visitors and the novelty of a new baby has passed, it's important for both partners to take care of themselves both mentally and physically. As routines and tiredness set in, so can a loss of identity and self-worth. If, like so many other parents, you have just moved to a new area and friends and relatives live some distance away, you may start to feel lonely. After the birth, oestrogen levels plummet and are replaced by floods of the mothering hormone, prolactin. These hormonal changes can lead to emotional mood swings which happen to almost every new mother and are commonly known as the baby blues. New mums may feel weepy, irritable or resentful toward their new lifestyle, fearful over their baby's health, tired or disappointed by their birth experience.

The early weeks of parenthood can have its ups and downs for partners too. Some research suggests that fathers can experience similar hormonal surges to mothers as well as feelings of neglect and exclusion as mother and child form their close bond. New dads may also question their ability as a father if this is their first child. Again, spend time with each other, make time to talk and try some of the suggestions below:

▶ *Keep in touch with other parents through toddler groups, arranged lunches, playgrounds, and exercise groups.*
▶ *Keep in touch with old friends.*
▶ *Treat yourself to a new hairstyle, outfit, beauty treatment or massage.*
▶ *Take time to be alone, go for a walk, have a bath, cup of tea, whatever, just take some time out even if it is just 15 minutes.*
▶ *Get it all out and have a good cry.*
▶ *Talk to a therapist or call a parent helpline.*

- *Try aromatherapy oils such as ylang-ylang, clary sage, geranium and rose in a bath, diffuser or as a massage in a carrier oil.*
- *Have a cup of lemon balm tea every morning with honey and a fresh slice of lemon.*
- *Try a combination of Bach flower remedies such as walnut, willow or cherry plum throughout the day.*
- *Increase your intake of vitamin B, C, calcium, magnesium and zinc through food intake or supplements.*
- *Get outside, lie in the park or garden with your baby or go for a walk together.*

Having a family can also take its toll on the relationship between you and your partner. Try to make sure that you set aside at least one night or day per week to be together and to talk to each other. If you do run into problems don't hesitate to seek the help of a relationship counsellor. You might feel a bit awkward about this, but the benefit of having someone to offload your problems onto and help you and your partner communicate with each other, is huge. You can even find subsidized or free counselling. Check out your local counsellors for details of the options they can give you.

POST-NATAL DEPRESSION (PND)

This is different from the baby blues and is defined as a 'profound and consistent lowering of mood' following childbirth. The symptoms are much more extreme than those of the baby blues to the point that some women are so distraught and confused that they don't realize the seriousness of their depression. Symptoms may include:

- *insomnia, disturbing dreams and problems getting out of bed*
- *loss of appetite or comfort eating*
- *weight loss or gain*
- *increased interest in alcohol, sedatives and other medication*
- *feeling sluggish, irritable, exhausted and unable to complete basic daily tasks*
- *difficulty concentrating and making decisions*

- ▶ *lack of interest in the baby, distracting oneself with other tasks to avoid dealing with the baby*
- ▶ *suicidal thoughts, fantasies of death or hurting oneself or the baby*
- ▶ *feelings of hopelessness, anxiety, panic*
- ▶ *mood swings and uncontrollable crying*
- ▶ *social withdrawal.*

Factors that may predispose a mother to PND may include severe hormonal changes, a previous history of mental illness, chronic fatigue, a sick baby or a traumatic birth experience and lack of support. Every woman is different and other factors may be involved. Whatever the reason, if you suspect you or your partner has PND seek medical advice as soon as possible. It is important to tell someone in order to get support as well as trying the suggested remedies for baby blues. There are now national helplines for PND sufferers and local programmes of support available through your doctor or midwife which may include counselling and help with childcare. In more extreme cases, a hospital stay is often exactly what a mother needs to gain some distance and perspective on what is happening in her life. It is a mother's right to speak out and get help for PND. Speaking about the condition can only help your family and many others understand and cope with the condition.

Green parent guide to after the birth

🍃 Get some help and have some time out after the birth before having visitors. Make sure you bond with your baby by breastfeeding (even if it's only for a few weeks) or having skin to skin contact whilst bottle feeding. Use a sling and sleep in the same room as your baby. Eat healthily and drink plenty of water. Make sure you get out for a walk every day or take up another form of exercise. Make sure you keep in contact with other mums and friends and don't hesitate to seek help if you're feeling low.

🌿🌿 As well as the tips above try attending baby massage classes. As well as being great for baby it's a good way to meet other parents. Try bathing with your baby and make sure both parents take time out for themselves as well as having special time for each other. Feeling rundown? Treat yourself to a massage. Try herbal teas and aromatherapy oils to aid healing.

🌿🌿🌿 Hire the services of a post-natal doula. Use attachment parenting methods to suit your needs. Mothers should try post-natal yoga classes and take some time out for regular massages or meditation. Partners should take as much care of baby as possible. Use the natural remedies suggested to heal the perineum if required. Learn to interpret the meaning of your baby's cries. Seek counselling for any emotional or relationship problems.

4

Food

In this chapter you will learn:

- *about breastfeeding*
- *how to get the most out of bottle feeding*
- *ways to wean*
- *how to feed your family as healthily, cheaply and conveniently as possible whilst helping to protect our environment.*

If you are a first-time parent you will probably have lots of questions about feeding your baby from birth until weaning time. There are, as usual, multitudes of options and the big corporate baby milk and food companies really want you to buy their products. Is this because formula milk is better for parents and baby? No, research has shown that breastfed babies have less tummy, breathing and ear infections than bottle-fed babies. Is it because it's cheaper? No, the average spend on formula milk and bottle feeding equipment until a child is one year old is approximately £400/US$900 compared to about £100/$250 for a breastfed baby. That's a saving of over £200/$500! Is it because it's more convenient? Well, any parent who's had to mess around with powder, bottles and sterilizers will probably tell you that it's a major pain. Questions over the sterility of formula milk that's pre-made and kept in the fridge may also mean that you'll have to make the milk up as and when you need it.

Whilst providing you with an apparently convenient and healthy feeding option for your child, the food giants are also making a tasty profit. Gone are the days when people thought that bottle feeding and mass produced baby mush was the modern way to go. Things have moved on since then and the super modern, trendy, healthy and cheap way to do things is to breastfeed! No mass-market food company should be deciding what you feed your baby and how you spend your money. Only you should do that, so here are a few pointers to get mothers started on the path to successful breastfeeding:

▶ *Start breastfeeding as soon as possible and don't introduce expressed milk in a bottle until breastfeeding is properly established (approximately six to eight weeks).*
▶ *Mums should make sure they are in a comfortable position and environment for feeding, using cushions for support if required.*
▶ *Get help with positioning from the start, asking your midwife or health visitor for advice.*
▶ *It may help mums to join a breastfeeding peer support group where they can swap stories and help each other.*
▶ *Breastfeeding should not be painful, so if it is, seek help and advice as soon as you can.*
▶ *Breastfeeding should be a pleasurable, bonding experience as each feed produces a rush of endorphins (or happy hormones) that make both mother and baby feel good and relieve stress.*

Fact

The World Health Organization recommends that babies need nothing other than breast milk for the first six months of life.

Breast is best

Breastfeeding:

▶ *aids the development of your baby's immune system*
▶ *helps your baby gain all the weight it needs after birth*
▶ *aids dental health*

- *could help children develop more quickly than bottle-fed ones and result in them being generally more intelligent in the long term*
- *decreases risk of stomach and digestive problems including allergies to cow's milk*
- *helps reduce the risk of your child developing asthma or eczema*
- *helps to protect the mother from cancers and arthritis*
- *boosts the mother's mental and physical health therefore reducing the likelihood of post-natal depression*
- *may protect the mother against type-2 diabetes*
- *is convenient and free*
- *helps mums get their figure back after birth as it encourages the uterus to shrink back to shape and uses 30 per cent of a woman's daily calorie intake*
- *makes you feel good knowing that you're giving your child the best possible start in life*
- *aids bonding*
- *avoids the use of formula milk, as its production is harmful to the environment and encourages conventional high yield dairy milk production, using needless amounts of energy in its manufacture and transportation.*

OVERCOMING THE TRICKY BITS

Some women do not want to breastfeed, cannot breastfeed or give up after a few weeks. There may be several reasons for this, such as pain, lack of support, low milk production or cultural bias against breastfeeding. Western society views breasts as sexual objects to be idolized and admired in glossy magazines, films and posters but is intolerant of breasts in public or in the media for any purpose other than sexual. This conditioning is so strong that many women themselves have come to view their breasts purely as sexual items with no other purpose. Some governments have now made it illegal to stop a woman from breastfeeding in public in an effort to turn attitudes around.

Old-fashioned ideas about child rearing and discipline which aim to make our children as independent as possible from a young age may also bias some parents against breastfeeding. Initially, breastfeeding should be baby led. Letting a baby cry it out at this stage is just not an option. Breast milk is far more digestible than formula milk, so breastfed babies require more regular feeding which may not fit in with the busy schedules of some parents. Women who are returning to work may be put off breastfeeding due to the attitude to breastfeeding mothers in the workplace and the inconvenience of having to express and store breast milk. It may take time to establish breastfeeding. Many women may mistake their subconscious mental attitudes and fears about their breasts and breastfeeding in public for problems with establishing breastfeeding and pain for the unfamiliarity of a new sensation.

If you or your partner can relate to any of these feelings please don't lose heart. The benefit you'll be bringing to your child is huge and you'll be helping to turn the tide of public opinion around to support breastfeeding. Likewise, if you choose not to breastfeed or cannot for any reason, it's important not to feel guilty or a failure. You have tried to do the best you possibly can for you and your baby and there are lots of ways that you can get the best out of bottle feeding too (see 'Getting the most out of bottle feeding' later in this chapter). Here are some tips to make breastfeeding easier:

▶ *Consider purchasing, hiring or borrowing an electric breast pump to help you and your partner to give your baby a bottle when required.*
▶ *Mums should sort out a private space at work to express milk and talk this over with any superiors to ensure they have their full support.*
▶ *Consider changing working hours to suit your needs.*
▶ *Mums should make sure they have lots of female support in the form of friends who've breastfed, breastfeeding advisors or a breastfeeding group such as La Leche League (see the Taking it further section for details), who have groups all over the world and operate on a regional as well as national basis.*

It's best to feed new born babies on demand as this makes sure enough milk is produced for the child's needs. It's also important for parents to follow their intuition as well as following prompts from their baby. The average baby feeds eight to twelve times a day during the first two weeks, decreasing to six to nine feeds during the second month. During the first month mums can feel that most of their time is spent breastfeeding. New mums should use this time to relax and enjoy the closeness with their baby. Mums should also drink plenty of water and maintain a healthy diet at all times but especially during breastfeeding. Remember that what a mum eats and drinks is transferred to her child through her breast milk. Breastfeeding mums should avoid excessive amounts of coffee and alcohol and avoid food additives and pharmaceutical drugs. They should completely eliminate smoking and recreational drugs.

Here are some natural solutions to breastfeeding problems:

- *Feed babies regularly to stimulate milk production.*
- *Use expressed breast milk to soothe cracked nipples (it's also good for baby's eye infections, cradle cap and dry skin).*
- *Warm baths can help mums to relax and their milk to let-down, as can essential oils and massage.*
- *Full, sore breasts or engorged breasts can be soothed with frequent feeding or expressing and a warm compress applied to the breast can help the milk to flow.*
- *Put cabbage leaves in the fridge (Savoy is best), cut a circle out of the middle for the nipple and score lightly with a sharp knife to release the juices in the leaf which are believed to have anti-inflammatory properties, then tuck them inside the bra to reduce swelling and absorb heat.*
- *Essential oils such as calendula and chamomile diluted in carrier oil can be used to soothe inflammation but care should be taken not to put them near the nipple or surrounding area.*

Getting the most out of bottle feeding

Some mums cannot feed for health reasons such as mastectomy, breast reduction, birth defects or hormone problems. Others simply choose not to. Whatever mums decide to do they should feel confidant and secure about their decision. Parents should always ensure that their decisions are informed ones! Here are some tips for getting the most out of bottle feeding your baby:

▶ *Have as much skin to skin contact whilst feeding baby as possible.*
▶ *Buy glass feeding bottles instead of plastic ones (from any of the numerous green parenting shops or websites) to avoid chemicals leaching into the milk.*
▶ *Look for organic or alternative infant formulas such as goat's milk formula which may be beneficial for babies who seem to have an allergy to cow's milk.*
▶ *Research the alternatives to milk as there may be some traditional homemade infant milk substitutes used by traditional cultures that may suit your baby, but these must be thoroughly researched and used at your own discretion.*
▶ *Get the nurturing hormone, prolactin, flowing for both parents by singing to your baby, baby massage, co-sleeping and baby wearing (carrying baby in a sling).*
▶ *Don't ever feel guilty about not breastfeeding a baby, but if you do, talk it over with friends or relatives or consult your GP for counselling and support, remembering to celebrate the things you can give your child rather than feeling bad about what you think you can't give.*

Six months and beyond

Feeding your baby conventional, jarred food may seem convenient but it's certainly not cheap and may not be offering your child the best start in life. Everyone needs a bit of a hand now and then with the odd jar but it is much better if you can prepare your own food for your baby as much as possible.

Feeding your child natural, healthy food from the beginning helps reduce the risks in later life of heart disease, obesity and anaemia as well as the more immediate ailments such as allergic reactions, asthma, eczema and behavioural problems. Jarred baby food doesn't contain as many vital nutrients as freshly prepared food and many contain unnecessary sugars and salts. Many companies use starches (often listed as rice starch on the label) and water to bulk out their meals which have no nutritional benefits to your child. You can buy organic jarred food but always check the label as jarred organic baby food made by the big, mass-market baby food companies doesn't always mean better quality. Always check the label! More and more companies (usually small cottage industries started by mums) now offer highly nutritious, freshly prepared, frozen baby food in handy cubes. If you're buying ready-made food for your baby opt for this kind or try to buy organic and avoid the big baby food companies.

Begin introducing solids to your baby (no earlier than six months of age) by mixing a little pure baby rice with the usual milk. As your baby becomes more adventurous try adding a little puréed fruit or veg to the mixture and, as she becomes more used to the new tastes and sensations you can vary the amounts.

Kids really love sweet vegetables such as parsnip, carrot, beetroot, sweet potato and butternut squash and you wouldn't believe some of the mixtures you can get away with. There's no need to add salt or sugar as foods naturally contain enough of these. Prepare food in bulk and freeze in ice cube trays to save time and effort. Try to steam food if possible (it keeps more of the nutrients in) then simply purée with a hand blender, pop it in ice cube trays and you've got enough to last you for a few weeks! If possible buy organic fruit, vegetables and baby rice.

Your baby's food should be natural, healthy and fun. Nothing beats fresh, basic homemade food that you can trust. As babies get older they enjoy helping in the kitchen. Playing with spoons, mixing lentils and just making a mess is an excellent way of spending time together and helping your child learn about texture, colour and where food comes from. To help get you started here

are a few favourite recipes donated by mum of two Clare Downer.
Enjoy hearty, homemade food but most of all, have fun!

Insight

Never give your child sugary drinks in a bottle or spouted cup.
They will rot her delicate milk teeth and give her a craving
for sugar.

Baked sweet butternut squash

1 medium butternut squash

2–4 tbsp freshly squeezed orange juice

Pinch of cinnamon (optional)

Preheat the oven to 180°C. Thoroughly wash the skin of the
squash and cut in half lengthways. Using a spoon, scoop out
the seeds and discard. Place on a baking tray skin side down
and fill the cavities with the orange juice. Sprinkle a little
cinnamon over the squash if desired and bake in the oven
for 50–60 minutes or until cooked through. Remove from
the oven and leave on the tray to cool for up to 30 minutes.
Tip the orange juice from the cavities into a bowl and peel
the skin from the squash (this should come away very easily.)
Mash or puree the squash with the orange juice, adding
water if required until you have the right consistency for
your baby.

This works really well for older babies or toddlers when
combined with some cooked brown rice, peas and a little
grated cheese.

Vegetable purée

1 potato

1 parsnip

1 carrot or 1 turnip

4 to 5 tablespoons of your baby's usual milk or water

Peel vegetable and dice. Steam for about ten minutes or until the vegetable is soft. Press through a sieve and mix with liquid. You can use a blender or food processor to purée the vegetables.

Mango mush

Serves: 2–3

1 dried apricot

2 tablespoons pure orange juice

1 small ripe mango

1 small ripe banana

Soak the apricot in the orange juice, and leave in the refrigerator overnight.

Slice the mango, remove the pit and then remove the flesh. Peel the banana and dice. Purée the apricot, mango and banana and, if required, thin with your baby's usual milk.

Dairy-free, sugar-free muffins

Makes: 8–12

150 g/3 oz plain flour

150 g/3 oz wholemeal flour

1 1/2 tsp baking powder

75 g/3 oz organic apple purée (can use maple syrup or honey for older children if preferred)

1 egg (egg substitute if required)

250 ml/8–9fl oz rice milk/goats milk

90 ml/3fl oz vegetable or sunflower oil

3–4 oz/150–175 g blueberries*

Preheat oven to 180°C. Sift the flours and baking powder together into a large mixing bowl, tipping any left over bran into the bowl. Add the apple purée, milk and oil, and mix until just combined – do not over mix! Carefully fold in the blueberries, or whatever you choose to use. Line a fairy cake tin with muffin cases, or rub some oil in each section of a muffin tin if preferred. Divide the mixture and bake in the oven for 12–18 minutes. Leave to cool in the tin for 10 minutes then transfer to a rack to completely cool.

*You can vary this recipe by choosing you own combination, or by substituting any of the following:

- ▶ *1 oz grated carrot combined with 3 oz canned crushed, drained pineapple*
- ▶ *3 oz grated apple combined with 1 oz plump raisins*
- ▶ *1 large skinned and chopped peach with 2 oz raspberries*
- ▶ *The zest of one lemon with 2–3 oz of sultanas.*

Mealtimes are fun, messy times and a great way to develop new skills. Here are some top tips for natural, healthy eating and stress-free mealtimes:

- *Avoid chemical additives, high salt, fat or sugar content, processed foods, genetically modified foods and mechanically reconstituted meat.*
- *Read the label to find out what's in the food and if in doubt leave it out.*
- *Try to use fruit as a snack, but avoid snacks just before mealtimes.*
- *Try to give your child five portions of fruit and vegetables every day.*
- *Only give your child water and her usual milk to drink for as long as possible and* never *give her sugary drinks in a bottle or spouted cup as this will rot her delicate milk teeth and give her a craving for sugar.*
- *When eating out, try to take your own food with you for your child especially if under three years old, as many restaurants don't provide high quality food for babies or children.*
- *Do not let mealtimes turn into a battle, so if your child refuses to eat a certain food, don't make an issue of it and simply re-introduce it at a later date.*
- *Don't offer older children substitutes for food they refuse to eat, instead offer them fresh fruit to eat later on, therefore setting good eating habits and a respect and appreciation of food.*
- *Try to eat together as a family as often as possible and use this time to chat, bond and enjoy each other's company.*
- *Prepare your own fresh food as often as possible and include children in the process as much as you can (see Chapter 9 for more ideas and suggestions).*

What does organic really mean?

Organic food is grown under guidelines which limit the use of genetically modified seeds and animal feeds, chemical pesticides, fertilizers and animal feed additives. Organic farming methods respect the environment by working in harmony with it rather than trying to control it. Growing food this way reduces the impact of farming on the environment and produces healthier, more natural food. Organic food generally contains fewer additives and preservatives, less added salt and refined sugar and no genetically modified ingredients. However it's always worth checking the label to be sure. Also, food should not have travelled too far to reach your plate.

FOOD MILES

This is the distance our food has to travel to reach our kitchen cupboard. The miles burn fuel which in turn produces carbon dioxide (CO_2), contributing to global warming. It's estimated that the ingredients for a typical Sunday lunch could have travelled up to 24,000 miles to get to our dinner plate! Our taste for exotic, out of season, cheap foods and our love affair with supermarket shopping has led to food being produced thousands of miles away to be transported to a processing plant in another country, to then be flown or shipped for sale in another continent on a supermarket shelf. Avoid contributing to exploitation of cheap labour and agriculture in developing countries and to carbon emissions. Purchase local or seasonal produce or grow your own. Don't be fooled into thinking organic food won't involve lots of food miles. It shouldn't, but it often does. Unscrupulous supermarkets like to sell packaged, overpriced organic food from overseas, when often it could be produced in our own country.

ADDITIVES

These are put into our food when it's being processed to preserve it, or to make it look better or taste better. Many of these additives also make us hooked on that particular food. Let's face it, which child doesn't love a good dose of sugar? Additives may include preservatives, artificial colouring, flavourings, preservatives and sweeteners. Some of these substances have been banned in certain countries as they have been found to cause cancers in laboratory animals. They can also cause dramatic behavioural changes such as hyperactivity, mood swings, sleeplessness, headaches and poor concentration in children as well as allergies, asthma, eczema, headaches, dizziness and seizures. Additives are found in almost every junk food marketed to children such as sweets, crisps, desserts, cereals, juices and drinks, snacks, birthday cakes, frozen and ready-made meals. Get informed and get armed! Read labels and try to avoid all additives. The ones listed below are particularly common ones that you really should avoid. Some of the colourings listed are actually banned in Austria, some European countries and the USA:

▶ **artificial sweeteners** – *sodium benzoate (E221), sulphur dioxide (E220), aspartame (E951), acesulfame K, tartrazine, homogenized fats*
▶ **artificial colourings** – *quinoline yellow (E104), sunset yellow E110, carmoisine red (E122), allura red (E129), indigo carmine (E132), brilliant blue (E133), brilliant black (E151), aluminium (E173)*
▶ **flavour enhancers** – *monosodium glutamate (MSG or E621), L-Glutamic acid (E620), disodium guanylate (E627), disodium inosinate (E631).*

GENETICALLY MODIFIED (GM) FOOD

This is food which has had its genes scientifically altered to make it more disease and pest resistant. Tomatoes, soya and maize are the most commonly genetically modified foods. There are concerns that these crops will only respond to their corresponding chemical pesticides and these are expensive. The selling of GM seed to developing countries with the apparent aim of drought-, pest- and disease-resistant crops is commendable, but not if these poor farmers are reliant on expensive pesticides made by large western corporations. Farmers would also be unable to save seeds from their crops for the following year as most of the offspring from GM crops are dormant. The full effects of cross pollination with non-GM and organic crops and the resulting effect on the livelihood of the farmer are not yet fully understood. Neither are the effects of GM food on human health. Most GM crops are intensively farmed, putting great pressure on wildlife habitats, soil, water and the environment as a whole.

Go organic. GM ingredients are not permitted in organic food. Boycott GM foods and check out your local supermarket's stance. GM foods should either be clearly labelled or not sold at all. Many supermarkets have stringent policies already in place, removing all GM foods from their shelves. If yours hasn't, put pressure on them to do so.

Look for the Soil Association stamp of organic certification. The Soil Association are one of the biggest regulating bodies of organic food and its production in the UK. They have banned the use of certain food additives in any product endorsed by them. Visit their website for more information at www.whyorganic.org. Every country has its own regulatory body for organic food and its certification. Check out which ones are used in your country. All organic certification bodies follow the same basic regulations but each country may add its own extra ones on top of these. The International Federation of Organic Agricultural Movements (IFOAM) www.ifoam.org, groups together 750 organic institutions worldwide and ensures that similar basic standards are maintained.

FAIR TRADE FOOD

Most supermarkets and health food shops also stock fair trade food and drink. Food produced in this way ensures that the people who grew and harvested it are given a fair wage and working conditions and not exploited by big companies who are only interested in profit. For more information on fair trade log on to: www.ethicalconsumer.org.

Here are some benefits of organic food:

- ▶ *It saves on food miles and the environment.*
- ▶ *It protects your family from the harmful chemicals used in non-organic food production such as artificial fertilizers, pesticides, fungicides, drugs and routine antibiotics.*

▶ *Purchasing organic food provides vital support to local and sustainable food production which is very important to farmers who now struggle to make a living from heavily subsidized conventional farming methods.*

▶ *You are helping to make a political and environmental statement for the future health of our children and the environment.*

▶ *You are helping to reduce the pollution to water courses caused by intensive farming.*

▶ *You are helping to protect the diversity of natural wildlife and habitats, as intensive farming strips the soil of resources and trees are removed to make way for large fields – organic agriculture keeps these natural resources in place, encouraging wildlife as a form of natural pest and disease control and fertilization.*

▶ *You are making sure your children have the healthiest and best possible start in life.*

▶ *Organic food tastes better, especially if it's also locally produced, as it's fresher and retains more of its nutrients, as well as being cheaper.*

▶ *You are making your own decisions, not ones based on expensive and persuasive corporate marketing, so this just has to have a feel good factor.*

Fact

Around 350 chemical pesticides are routinely used in conventional farming and residues are often present in non-organic food. The Soil Association allows just four substances to be used for pest control.

HOW AND WHERE CAN I BUY ORGANIC FOOD EASILY AND CHEAPLY?

Organic supermarket food can be convenient but more expensive. A cheaper way to buy organic food is from farm shops, market stalls and local fruit, vegetable and butcher's shops.

Many farms also run box schemes. This means you can have a selection of organic produce delivered in a box to your door. Some companies even offer an online order service. All these options also have the added advantage of no fancy packaging or additives, just good wholesome food you can trust. You'll also be giving much needed business and support to local farmers and your community! If cost is an issue, buy in bulk through a food co-operative, or alternatively, prioritize your needs. Only buy a few organic items each week which are most vulnerable to chemical contamination. These are generally anything you eat raw, such as fruit and salad vegetables. Meat, milk and eggs are also good items to buy organically.

Here are some ways to keep your family's food green:

▶ *Include as much freshly prepared, organic food in your children's lunch boxes as you can, which is healthy, cost saving and low on packaging too.*
▶ *Go vegetarian or vegan as it's healthy, cheap and the production of vegetables, fruit, nuts, beans and pulses uses much less energy and resources than the production of meat.*
▶ *Grow your own.*
▶ *Prioritize needs by thinking about which foods are luxuries and which are essentials, then cut down on luxuries and use the money saved to buy organic, fair trade food.*
▶ *Choose super foods which provide large doses of essential nutrients that help to boost immune systems, cleanse the body of toxins and generally boost health, such as lemons, beetroot, blueberries, oats, apples, almonds, carrots, seeds, sprouted seeds, mushrooms, broccoli, grapes, garlic and onions (see Taking it further section for recommended books on this subject).*
▶ *Eat fresh, raw or steamed food which retains many more nutrients than boiling, frying or baking.*
▶ *Lower fish, meat and dairy consumption, as in most developed countries we eat much more than we need, a contributing factor to obesity and heart disease.*

- One or two portions of meat and one portion of fish per person per week provides enough protein and you can boost protein levels with a selection of nuts, beans and pulses.
- Shop around for good deals and bargains, check local producers and see if they'll do you a deal on regular orders of goods such as eggs and milk.
- Haggle for bargains at your local farmers' market.
- Join a food co-op to buy organic, fair trade, dry or tinned goods and chemical free household products at wholesale prices.
- Sign up for a local box scheme in order to get fresh, local organic food delivered straight to your door.
- Buy farm gate produce and support local producers.
- Try to shop for seasonal or locally grown food, especially when supermarket shopping.
- Prepare your own food as much as possible.
- Encourage schools and nurseries to follow healthy eating policies using freshly grown, organic food where possible.
- Avoid GM foods.
- Campaign for tighter regulation on food additives, food trade and production by lobbying politicians to take action.
- Read and understand food labels.
- Teach children about food marketing and branding that is aimed squarely at them and encourage them to make their own healthy choices.
- Buy books to inform you about cooking with seasonal vegetables and using the natural nutrients in foods to keep your family healthy.

Green parenting guide to food

Breastfeed for as long as possible. Try cooking homemade food for you and your baby as much as you can. Can't cook? Many local community centres and initiatives offer free or subsidized cooking classes, a great opportunity to have a bit of a laugh and meet other parents. Try buying one organic product every week such as meat or eggs and see how it goes.

🌿🌿 Try a local box scheme. If it is too expensive halve the cost by sharing with a neighbour or friend. Choose to buy a few organic products regularly and try to buy local or national produce over imported organic foods. Check labels to see where they've come from.

🌿🌿🌿 Buy fair trade and organic food as often as you can. Start a food co-operative and buy in bulk from a wholesaler to reduce cost. Try to buy local produce where possible and lobby your local supermarket to carry more organic and fair trade lines as well as putting pressure on companies to label all ingredients. Try to eat what's in season and don't forget the organic booze!

5

....

Nappies

In this chapter you will learn:
- *how to choose nappies to suit your lifestyle*
- *how to save money by using alternatives to disposable nappies*
- *about handy green nappy changing tips.*

_____

Cloth nappies

Fancy saving up to £1,000 (US$2,000) this year? It's very simple, just use cloth nappies. Not only will you be saving money but you'll be doing your bit toward helping the environment too.

Eighteen billion disposable nappies are placed in landfill sites each year because disposable nappies are a single use item for which there is no clean and convenient method of disposal. The average family spends approximately £1,200 (US$2,350) on disposable nappies for each child until they are potty trained. But where do the used nappies go? They're collected with the rest of our rubbish and put into a big hole in the middle of our beautiful countryside called a landfill site, often with the contents still inside the nappy. As many as 100 viruses can survive in soiled nappies for up to two weeks! The only place for raw sewage is down the toilet (or compost toilet if you're super green).

I try to use as many natural products as possible and would probably have used real nappies anyway but I became very sensitive to perfumes and chemicals in all products when I was pregnant. Along with the smell of dirty disposables and the thought of adding to the landfill problem, exposing my baby to the perfumes and gels in disposable nappies wasn't an option. Years ago I had practice at changing my baby cousin's terry nappies so I had no fear of the unknown when folding nappies and using pins on wriggly babies. Now there are plenty of fitted nappy designs to choose from and I would try shaped terries, even though I admit to enjoying the ritual of using terry squares (you've got to take your fun where you can get it!). For me the only thing about using real nappies that I didn't like was storing nappy buckets, but this was far outweighed by the fact I never ran out of nappies and didn't have to run to the shops to buy more. A warning – baby's first dirty nappies are pretty messy with meconium. It's not much fun to get out but don't let it put you off, it gets easier, or avoid it by using environmentally friendly disposables for the first week or so.

Mother of two, Helen O'Gorman, Fife

Getting rid of disposable nappies has become such a challenge to local authorities that there has even been talk of taxing their sale. Due to the successful marketing campaigns by the manufacturers of disposable nappies, some people now believe that the laundering of cloth nappies is just as bad for the environment as using disposables. However the Landbank Report concluded that compared to cloth nappies, disposable nappies use twenty times more raw materials, three times more energy, twice as much water and generate sixty times more waste.

The damage done to the environment is only one factor in the choice between cloth nappies, disposables or a mixture of both. The other factor is the health and comfort of your baby. A baby's skin is much thinner than adults' and absorbs much of what it comes in contact with. Disposable nappies contain super absorber granules which are made of a chemical which swells to absorb the urine. They also contain dioxins, a bi-product of paper bleaching. Why expose your child to unnecessary chemicals when you don't have to? Further advantages of using cloth nappies include:

▶ *Disposables are not as breathable as a cloth nappy so they raise the temperature of the testes and scrotum, which has been linked to effects on fertility by a German study. However, further conclusive research is required.*
▶ *Babies in cloth nappies tend to be changed more frequently keeping them drier and helping to avoid nappy rash.*
▶ *Babies wearing cloth nappies may potty train quicker than those wearing disposables as they can feel when they are wet.*

Anyone who's used sanitary or personal care products will know how uncomfortable they can be. Just imaging having to wear something like that for up to three years and you'd probably opt for natural cotton and silk too!

Facts

'Around 80 per cent of a used nappy and its content are biodegradable.' Absorbent Hygiene Product Manufacturers Association (AHPMA)

'We are sharing our planet with part of every disposable nappy ever put into a landfill site.' BabyGROE

> 'Disposable nappies form four per cent of all household waste in the UK, costing the tax payer £40 million pounds per year to dispose of them.' National Association of Nappy Services (NANS)
>
> 'Disposable nappies use 3.5 times more energy to produce than real nappies, 8 times more non-renewable materials and 90 times more renewable resources.' The Nappy Lady

Imagine 18 billion dirty nappies getting transported to landfill sites everyday! Local councils are getting worried as landfill sites are becoming full and they're running out of space. But you want the convenience of a disposable nappy and you're about to change roughly 5,480 nappies until your baby is potty trained so what are the choices? Cloth nappies have come a long way since the days of pins, terry squares and crinkly plastic waterproof pants. Despite the publicity claiming that cloth nappies are no better for the environment than disposable nappies, if you want to be in control of your baby's chemical environment then cloth nappies are the way to go. Remember you could spend up to £1,200 (US$2,355) on disposables. Here's how to start saving.

Cost comparison

Cheapest option with a saving of up to £1,000 (US$2,000).	Terry squares, fleece reusable nappy liner or flushable liners. Nappy Nippas to hold the nappies on and a good quality, soft, waterproof pant that grows with your baby.	Terry squares are great because they're cheap, they dry fast and they grow with your baby. Just pop the poo down the toilet with the liner and pop the nappy in a nappy bucket. When you've got a full load put the whole lot in the washing machine. Good quality waterproof pants that *(Contd)*

		grow with your baby will mean you don't need too many pairs, and they'll keep the wettest baby dry at night with a booster pad. A bit tricky to do the folding at first but by the end you'll be able to afford a family holiday for four!

Cost benefits

Medium saving of up to £800 (US$1,570) depending on combination used.	Shaped or pre-folded cloth nappies with same liners and pants as for terry squares or all-in-one nappies.	These are great for mums on the go. No need for folding or Nappy Nippas, these have poppers or Velcro. All-in-ones have the nappy and the waterproof pants all sewn together so it's a bit like a disposable but made of cloth, washable and without any chemicals. We found that the downside of all-in-ones is that they can take quite a long time to dry and that some brands have a tendency to leak. A lot of mums keep a few handy for when they're out and about.

Cost can be almost the same as disposable nappies depending on the local authority offer subsidies.	Nappy laundry service or biodegradable disposable nappies.	The great thing about a nappy laundry service is that you don't have to do anything but put the nappies on and take them off. They usually come as the pre-fold style and every week or more your specially designed nappy bin is collected and you're provided with a fresh stash of clean nappies. Biodegradable disposable nappies contain far fewer chemicals than normal disposable nappies and, under the right conditions, should break down within eight weeks. These are probably the most costly option but they're handy if you're out and about and can come in at roughly the same price as normal disposable nappies.

Many supermarkets now stock biodegradable nappies, cloth nappies, biodegradable liners, flushable, chemical-free wipes as well as a range of chemical-free nappy change toiletries for babies' delicate bottoms. There are all sorts of sizes, shapes and colours of nappies and wraps out there too so you can find something that suits your lifestyle and your baby.

Contact your local authority to see if they run a cloth nappy incentive scheme or can provide information. Alternatively, contact any of the companies you find in this book who'll give you unbiased parent to parent advice and reduced price trial packs. It's also a good idea to see what kind of nappies your local hospital is using and if necessary, take your own along to the hospital with you.

The whole thing can be a bit bewildering, so to help you make the right decision and prioritize your needs just ask yourself the following questions:

- *Is your main concern saving money, helping the environment, convenience, your child's health or a combination of all of these things?*
- *Is this your first child? If not you probably already have some ideas about what you want and may even have some nappies left over from the first time round.*
- *What kind of facilities do you have for drying nappies?*
- *Will your baby be in regular childcare and will your provider accept the use of reusable nappies (unbelievably some don't)?*
- *How do you feel after the birth? If you've had surgery, complications or a difficult birth your priority may be convenience.*
- *What is your budget? How much can you afford to spend now or would it be easier to spread the cost?*

NAPPY RASH

This is often wrongly associated with cloth nappies. According to an independent study on infants with 'very bad' and 'quite bad' nappy rash, 'The type of nappy worn did not emerge as a significant factor. Therefore, and contrary to widespread belief, disposable nappies seem to have little protective effect.' (Research conducted by Professor Jean Golding of Bristol University). However if your baby gets a sore bottom, here are some ways to help ensure a speedy recovery and avoid a repeat performance:

- *Avoid acidic foods in your baby's diet (and the mother's diet if she's breastfeeding) such as fruit juice and oranges.*
- *Allow your child to roam around nappy-free as much as possible.*
- *Avoid using fragranced baby wipes and creams as these may aggravate nappy rash, instead use a plain cotton flannel and warm water.*
- *Avoid petroleum based nappy creams or those which create a waterproof barrier on the skin and seal in the moisture instead of keeping it out. Try calendula cream instead or use a little expressed breast milk on the affected area and allow it to dry naturally.*
- *Change your baby's nappy as soon as it gets dirty.*

Elimination timing

This is the ultra green way to go. It involves realizing and getting into synch with your baby's natural toilet cycles so that you know when he needs the toilet. Holding your baby comfortably and securely over his potty on a regular basis gets him used to the familiar sounds and positions of going to the toilet and he'll soon learn to associate them with his potty. This is the method used in most traditional cultures for as long as records show and it works. It's cheap, cost free, waste free and encourages understanding and bonding between parent and child. It may take time and patience and a few mishaps but just imagine it, no nappies, ever!

Elimination timing can begin at birth and is usually started before six months of age. The terms 'Elimination Communication' and 'Natural Infant Hygiene' were coined by Ingrid Bauer and are used interchangeably in her book, *Diaper Free! The Gentle Wisdom of Natural Infant Hygiene* (2001).

There are no right or wrong choices, but it's your right to make an informed decision, so don't be swayed by all those cute adverts for the best nappies in the world. Only you can be the judge of that.

Wherever your journey of discovery takes you, you'll feel happier knowing your choice was an informed one. Bum Voyage!

Green parenting guide to nappies

🍃 Save money! Try a reusable nappy trial pack. Nobody is asking you to hand wash them, just pop them in the machine. Check out your local council to see if they can offer you more information or incentives. You could even just try using a cloth nappy some of the time.

🍃🍃 Use a laundry service if time is an issue. Combine real nappies with a more environmentally friendly disposable when you're out and about or at night. Try to use a gentle more environmentally friendly non-bio washing powder and biodegradable nappy sacks and wipes.

🍃🍃🍃 Use a real nappy system that suits your needs in combination with biodegradable or reusable liners, eco-friendly detergents and you could even try making your own nappy wipes. When washing, always make sure you have a full load and never wash at more than 40°C. Deodorize your nappy bucket with a few drops of tea tree oil and use bicarbonate of soda added to the water as an alternative to conventional nappy soak, it's much cheaper. Try to air dry your nappies where possible as the bleaching effect of the sun will keep them white and you'll save on your electricity bill if you don't tumble dry. Add a cup of white vinegar to the end of the wash as a natural fabric conditioner. Try elimination timing.

6

Keeping it clean

In this chapter you will learn:
- *about the chemicals in toiletries and cleaning products*
- *which chemicals to avoid*
- *how to keep your family and house naturally clean.*

Toiletries

Midwives recommend that babies are bathed in nothing
but water at birth and many other skin specialists are now
recommending that this be extended even longer. When your
baby is born his skin is completely and utterly brand new. You
will marvel at how soft and delicate his tiny hands are. Babies
are perfect and no matter what they smell like, they will always
be perfect.

There has been a sharp rise in skin and respiratory ailments such
as asthma and eczema, and research is starting to indicate that it
might just be something to do with what we put in and on our
bodies. Consider that our skin absorbs approximately 60 per cent
of everything it comes into contact with and that a baby's skin
is around six times thinner and five times more sensitive
than adults'.

So why do we seem obsessed with putting chemicals on our babies
and our own skin when we don't really need it? It's probably a

combination of habit and a lack of information about what's in the products we're using, but you and your baby's life wouldn't collapse if you stopped using them and your pocket would have more pennies in it!

Lots of big companies are getting larger because of our obsession with smelling of different aromas and cleaning things. When you're hit with the expense of a new baby, having to buy various baby toiletries is yet another extra cost that you could really do without. Don't wash babies in anything but water. Olive oil on cotton wool works wonders as a cleaner and moisturizer. If you really have to give your baby a good scrub, try buying organic, chemical free toiletries and use them rarely and sparingly.

Fact

Over 30,000 chemicals are currently produced in quantities over one tonne per year within the EU alone. Only a handful of these chemicals have been assessed for the risks they pose.

Greenpeace

Whether you think it's all a load of rubbish or not, it's your right to find out the facts and make a decision based on what you think rather than what all those fancy adverts make you feel. Besides, there are now more and more great businesses that produce toiletries without chemicals which smell lovely and are very competitively priced with other leading brands. You can also get them in your supermarket now. When shopping for toiletries don't believe it is pure just because it says it is on the label. Have a look at the ingredients and if in doubt, don't buy it.

Insight

A little honey, yoghurt and oatmeal combined can provide a very invigorating facial scrub.

Commonly used chemicals

The chemicals below have all been connected with various ailments and side effects through laboratory observations and inconclusive reports and studies. Some of these include cancers, liver complaints, problems with the nervous system, respiratory complaints and skin disorders:

▶ *paraben, a food grade preservative*
▶ *aluminium compounds (suggestions that they are carcinogenic but as yet no conclusive scientific evidence)*
▶ *urea, a preservative*
▶ *Sodium Lauryl Sulphate (SLS), a strong detergent*
▶ *Ammonium Laureth Sulphate, a coconut-derived detergent which is milder than SLS*
▶ *Phthalates, a group name for chemicals used as solvents and fragrance enhancers in certain cosmetics*
▶ *AHAs and Retinol A, so-called miracle anti-ageing ingredients*
▶ *synthetic fragrances, that may contain between 50 to 100 chemical ingredients*
▶ *artificial musks, absorbed through skin, which may cause liver damage and interfere with brain activity*
▶ *triclosan, used as an antibacterial*
▶ *DEA (diethanolamine), used as a solvent and detergent*
▶ *TEA (triethanolamine), a frequently used dispersing agent and emulsifier*
▶ *petrochemicals (including mineral oil and propylene glycol), used in creams.*

Alternatives for the whole family

You can purchase most of the ingredients below in your health food store, on the Internet or at your local pharmacy.

Sanitary care	Choose unbleached sanitary protection or reusable towels. There are now reusable menstrual devices on the market called menstrual cups which safely collect the menstrual flow.
Moisturizers	Try alternatives such as olive oil, coconut oil or blends of essential oil. Breast milk also nourishes skin and brings relief to dry skin conditions.
Hair care	Coconut oil can be used as a leave in, wash out conditioner. You can also make shampoo from boiled soap nuts. Use plant-based hair dyes or henna.
Toothpaste	Regular dental care is an essential preventative measure. Choose mercury-free fillings. Use fluoride and chemical-free toothpaste and natural bristle brushes made of wood.
Talcum powder	Cornflour is a silky soft and completely natural substitute free from harsh perfumes and skin dehydrating chemicals.
Deodorant	Crystal deodorant stones. Chemical-free deodorants.
Cosmetics	Try cutting down, buying chemical free or making your own.
Soap	Buy naturally scented soaps made from beeswax or plant derivatives. Make your own from soap nut shells.
Sunscreen	Only expose your family to moderate sun by covering up and staying in the shade. Use chemical-free, plant-based sun block.
Toner	Use a mixture of two parts rose water and one part witch hazel blended together in an atomizer.
Bath soak	One spoonful of Epsom salts makes a great soak. Make your own bath bombs

| | with 3 tablespoons of bicarbonate of soda, 1½ tablespoons of citric acid and a few drops of essential oil. Mix well and mould together with a drop of water. Store in a plastic bag. An oatmeal soak also provides essential oils. Put a handful of oats in an old stocking or muslin bag and leave to soak in the bathwater. |
| **Perfume** | Essential oils and 100 per cent natural vegan perfumes are a healthy alternative. |

Household cleaning products

Who can stand those adverts aimed at women for hygiene products and ultimate performance household cleaning products? Who really wants to spend their precious time or money worrying how white their whites are? Does whiter mean cleaner? Colorants, synthetic scents and optical brighteners are all used to give a fresh, clean impression but they are a real burden to the environment and may even cause health problems. Traces of these substances attach to fabric during washing and are then transferred to our skin through contact. This can increase the chances of skin irritation and allergies.

Petroleum-based surfactants (detergents) used in most of these products come from a non-renewable source and biodegrade much more slowly than vegetable based ones. During degradation they form compounds that are more dangerous than the original chemicals themselves. Some European governments have been discussing strategies to enforce manufacturers of household cleaning products to inform consumers about what chemicals are present in their products, but for now, manufacturers pretty much have free rein to use whatever they want.

Bleaches contained in household products make their way into our water courses, damaging wildlife and preventing waste and sewerage from breaking down properly. The most common ingredient in multi-purpose cleaners (up to 90 per cent) is water and then, more often than not, there is the non-recyclable packaging. Both are a waste of time, energy, resources and above all, your money!

There are lots of companies who provide gentler, more natural cleaning products. You'll also find them stocked at your local health food shop and most supermarkets now carry at least one range of environmentally friendly cleaning products.

Laundry balls are another alternative to conventional washing powders. You place them in the washing machine instead of detergent. Together they are supposed to produce ionized oxygen that activates the water molecules naturally and allows them to penetrate deep into clothing fibres to lift dirt away. They are reusable for over 1,000 washes and there are no harsh chemicals so cause less pollution. However, there are varying reports on how effective they are.

Soap nuts are a biodegradable alternative to laundry detergents. They are harvested sustainably in India and Nepal where they have been used as a traditional cleaning agent for years. They contain saponin, a natural soap. They can also be boiled up to make a soap base which can be used as shampoo and hand and body soap.

There are lots of natural alternatives to use as cleaning products such as vinegar for fabric softener or tea tree oil mixed with water as a natural disinfectant.

Essential ingredients for natural cleaning:

- *distilled white vinegar*
- *bicarbonate of soda*
- *soda crystals*
- *borax*
- *epsom salts*

- *household salt*
- *lemon juice makes things smell nice and is a natural bleaching agent; rind makes things sparkle*
- *tea tree oil*
- *lavender oil*
- *beeswax for polishing wood and floors.*

Window cleaner	Five parts water to one part vinegar in a recycled spray bottle. Much cheaper than window cleaner.
Toilet cleaner	Leave some vinegar down the toilet over night and flush the next day for a sparkly toilet bowl. Give the toilet a quick brush once a day to cut down on the need for toilet cleaners.
Bleach	Use neat lemon juice on the affected area or leave to soak overnight for really stubborn stains.
Fabric freshener	Use dried lavender or wax lavender beads in cupboards to keep clothes smelling nice.
Scourers	Use baking soda, it won't scratch delicate surfaces.
Floor cleaner	Add some grated soap to hot water and baking powder. Rinse with a water or vinegar solution for extra sparkle.
Fungicide	Mix clove or tea tree essential oil with water and dispense from a spray bottle to kill the mould on shower curtains and on tile grout.
Dishwasher powder	Mix bicarbonate soda with borax and fresh lemon or lemon oil to make homemade dishwasher powder.

The above ingredients can be used for numerous handy household and cleaning chores. You really don't need to buy conventional cleaning products at all and it works out to be much cheaper.

These are just a few recipes to get you started but you can find many more in specialist books or online.

Green parenting guide to keeping it clean

🍃 Even if you think it's a load of rubbish, just think of the money you could save by cutting down on a few cleaning products and toiletries. Your baby is gorgeous without artificial smells and he'll be clean enough with a good wash in warm water. Invest in a natural soap for occasional use and consider using olive oil as a natural moisturizer (test on a small area of skin first) but if you really must stick with the scented products, make sure you wash them off skin and surfaces really thoroughly!

🍃🍃 Try to buy natural toiletries and cleaning products when possible and use small amounts occasionally to make them last, especially if on babies and sensitive skin. Switch to using non-bleached sanitary products, say no to aerosol sprays and avoid deodorants containing aluminium.

🍃🍃🍃 Always try to use natural toiletries and cleaning products. Start campaigning to get the big companies to change what they put in their products. Make your own cleaning products and toiletries. Invest in some good guides. Buy recycled non-bleached toilet paper. Use soap nuts and laundry balls.

7

Health

In this chapter you will learn:
- *how to get the best out of the health service*
- *how to keep your family naturally healthy*
- *about child vaccination.*

Healthcare options

We all hope our babies will always be bouncing with vitality and health but there are always the inevitable bumps, bruises and childhood ailments. Knowing about your healthcare options in advance can save a lot of stress. There are a bewildering array of lotions, potions, supplements, medical aids and also complementary therapies. It can all get a bit confusing, especially if you are new to the job. Again, the key is to keep it simple and ask around to see what other people recommend. Buy a few books to keep you informed and use as a reference guide, and never feel afraid to ask your GP lots of questions. Many surgeries now have GPs who have trained in complementary therapies or who can refer you to a good therapist.

There are many natural remedies for the usual childhood illnesses. Some of these are detailed below.

HEADACHES

Drink lots of water. Apply a dot of tiger balm to the temples (only for adults and older children). You can buy this in most health food shops.

COUGHS

Bryonia homeopathic remedy, in pilule or tincture form, is good for coughs. Alternatively, make your own cough syrup. Steep one ounce of thyme leaf (from a herbalist or health food shop) in a cup of boiling water. Cool, strain and mix with a heaped dessert spoon of honey. Decant into a glass jar. Refrigerate and use as required.

RESPIRATORY PROBLEMS

For babies, use an aromatherapy vaporizer. Pine, eucalyptus and thyme are all good oils for breathing problems. For adults and older kids, fill a big glass bowl with boiling water. Add one of the following: menthol crystals, tiger balm, tea tree or the essential oils mentioned above. Even better are dried eucalyptus leaves if you can get them. Allow the water to cool slightly then place head over the bowl (not too close or it'll burn). Place a towel over both head and bowl to trap vapours. Breathe deeply.

HAY FEVER

Coat the inside of the nose with a barrier to the allergen such as olive oil. Eat local honey for two months before the season starts, the theory being that you'll become desensitized.

CYSTITIS

Eat/drink cranberries in any form and lots of them as well as lots of water. Avoid acidic food and drink.

THRUSH

Take Acidophilus capsules. Eat natural live yoghurt and also apply this to the infected area. Tea tree oil and bergamot essential oil mixed with carrier oil and applied to the affected area will sooth itching. Avoid sugary and sugar-producing foods such as wheat and dairy.

DIGESTIVE COMPLAINTS

Eat cooked short-grain brown rice. Drink peppermint tea.
Take ginger in any form. Avoid fats, sugars and acids.

CHICKEN POX

Tepid baths with bicarbonate of soda added to water soothes
itching. Rhus tox homeopathic remedy is good for soothing
skin irritations.

SORE THROATS

Take the homeopathic remedy Heper Sulp. Drink sage or
thyme tea.

COLDS

It's important not to suppress a cold and to allow it to work
its way out of the system. Pulsatilla is known as an effective
homeopathic remedy for treating colds and mucus build up. Try
a hot drink of boiled water, freshly squeezed lemon juice, honey,
crushed garlic clove and a teaspoon of grated ginger. Mix together
and allow to infuse as it cools. This will help ease symptoms and
work the cold through the body. It sounds horrible but if taken at
the early onset of the cold, it really works. Disguise the garlic taste
with plenty of honey. Add a touch of chilli if accompanied with
a fever. This eases inflammation and helps work the fever out of
the body. You'll be unlikely to get this remedy near the kids!
Take plenty of rest and fluids.

EARACHE

Warmth applied to the ear in the form of a hot water bottle or
heat pad eases pain. Olive or mullein oil, gently warmed and a few
drops applied into the ear on a piece of cotton wool or by pipette
can help liquefy wax build up and ease pain.

FEVER

High temperatures are the body's natural defence mechanism and a cleansing of unwanted bacteria and infection. Dry fevers are dangerous but wet fevers are the body's healing tool. Rest and take as much fluid as possible. Allow young babies to drink as much milk as they want during a fever. If the temperature won't come down take a warm bath or shower and sponge down. Dab lightly dry and dress in thin clothing. Allow lots of fresh air into the room. Loss of appetite is usual. Call a doctor if the fever persists or is excessively high as there can be a risk of febrile fits in young babies.

CROUP

See 'respiratory problems' above. Spongia homeopathic remedy can be used for croup.

ECZEMA

Avoid petroleum-based and steroid-based creams, soaps, scented products and detergent-based laundry products. Try eliminating dairy, wheat, refined sugar and acid-forming foods from your child's diet. Instead, introduce foods which are known to help soothe skin conditions such as oats, hemp seed or oil and other foods rich in omega-3 fatty acids. Try an oat bath soak and ensure that bedrooms are well ventilated at night and bedclothes and nightwear are natural organic cotton if possible. Keep the sufferer as calm as possible and remove any source of stress from daily life. Use the same diet tips for asthma sufferers and consult a homeopath for a more in-depth holistic consultation.

HEAD LICE

Use tea tree based herbal shampoo as a deterrent or add tea tree oil to hair rinse. Regular brushing with a fine comb also acts as a deterrent. Avoid chemical-based products (organophosphates) and try any of the natural treatments now available online and in health food shops for severe infestations.

MEASLES

Allow time for lots of rest, recuperation and parental attention. See the 'fever' section above.

TEETHING

Homeopathic remedies chamomilla and Pulsatilla. Amber teething necklaces can be worn to comfort teething tots. Amber is believed to be a natural analgesic (painkiller). You can find these in most green parenting web shops. Herbal powders such as Ashton and Parsons also help.

NAPPY RASH

Please refer to Chapter 5.

To vaccinate or not to vaccinate

One of the biggest and most confusing decisions you'll have to make as a parent is whether to have your child vaccinated against a number of serious diseases including polio, mumps, measles, meningitis and diphtheria. With so many conflicting news reports in the media about the side effects of immunizing programmes and inconclusive research it can be difficult to come to a definitive decision about vaccinations.

Vaccination programmes aim to provide individuals with an immunity against serious infectious diseases and so create the widespread control of the disease through herd or group immunity. In other words, if nobody has it we can't spread it. However, critics argue that many serious diseases have been controlled through improved sanitation and better levels of hygiene rather than solely through vaccination.

Immunization through vaccination or inoculation works by injecting a weak form of a disease into the bloodstream. The body then creates antibodies to fight off the disease. The memory of these antibodies stays in the body, ready to fight off any future attacks of the disease. In most countries people have a choice about whether to vaccinate their children but in some countries it's a regulation which can result in children being excluded from nurseries and schools.

Many people believe that combined vaccines administered to babies as young as two months old, and then repeated as a programme of immunization through the first year of a child's life, are an overload to its immature immune system. Others believe that by injecting a disease into the bloodstream and bypassing the body's natural immune system response, the antibodies created are different from those of a natural reaction. This questions the effectiveness of the manufactured antibodies in the event of a real infection. Vaccines also contain a variety of chemicals, such as mercury and aluminium, as well as animal and bird cells, which is unacceptable to some parents.

However, the crux of the debate and the recent media attention has focused on the issue of chronic ailments as a result of immunization. These include eczema, asthma, diabetes and allergies with the main concern being autism.

Governments spend millions on advertising campaigns to encourage people to have their children immunized but offer little information about the alternatives to it. In response to this many groups now exist to disseminate research and information regarding the vaccination debate.

There really don't seem to be any rights or wrongs here and it is a very personal decision. Take your time and research as much as possible. Speak to doctors, health visitors, friends and a homeopath about their experiences and the alternatives available. Write down a list of pros and cons as you discover more information. Remember that you can choose to have your child immunized at any time or to have single rather than combined vaccines, so perhaps waiting until your child's immune system is more mature (approximately two years) would be a good option for you.

Whether you decide to vaccinate, to wait or to avoid it completely, follow these simple guidelines to offer your child the best natural protection against disease as possible:

▶ *Inform yourself about the symptoms of various diseases so that if your child does become ill she has the best chance possible of a quick diagnosis, treatment and recovery.*
▶ *If your child becomes ill create time to nurse her, allowing her body to work the illness out, therefore strengthening the immune system.*
▶ *Breastfeed your baby for as long as possible.*
▶ *Seek the advice of a homeopath or complementary therapist to ensure that you have alternative support.*
▶ *Don't create a sterile environment for your children – let them get dirty and battle the germs themselves as it all helps develop their immune system.*
▶ *Make sure children get plenty of exercise and fresh air.*
▶ *Follow a fresh, healthy whole-food diet, perhaps introducing super foods known to boost the immune system.*
▶ *Avoid the routine use of antibiotics, only using them when your child really needs them.*

Natural alternatives

All too often we find ourselves running to the doctor and ending up with antibiotics or a strong medicine for minor complaints. Try to avoid taking these and opt for a natural alternative after consultation with your GP. For everyday bumps and bruises it's a good idea to stock up with a first aid box full of as many natural treatments as possible. The guide below will help you start your own green first aid box. Remember that these are only suggestions and you can tailor the box to suit your family.

The green first aid box

Arnica cream: treats bumps, bruises and reduces swelling.

Arnica homeopathic pillules: bruises and shock.

Belladonna homeopathic pillules: fever, inflammation and onset of infection.

Chamomilla homeopathic pillules: teething babies.

Nux vomica homeopathic pillules: hangovers, indigestion, vomiting, colds, nerves and irritability.

Rescue remedy: for shock and distress, put a few drops on the tongue.

Chamomile tea: eye wash for conjunctivitis, soothing when drunk.

Aloe vera: fresh plant is better but in the form of a gel is also good for burns, abrasions and any skin problems, a powerful healer.

Raw honey: soothing, healer both internally and externally.

Lavender oil: inhaled can calm and aid sleep, works wonders applied diluted to minor skin burns.

Tea tree oil: powerful antiseptic, use dilute on cuts and sores or for head lice.

Oats: used as a bath soak for skin conditions.

Echinacea: taken as a tincture, boosts the immune system.

Ginger: taken as a tonic, boosts circulation.

Feverfew: for headaches (and migraines if taken daily).

Ginko bilboa: for poor circulation, also believed to help tinnitus.

Complementary therapies can be used to complement conventional medicine or on their own to help with everything from bruising, teething and colic to labour, back pain and breech births. There are so many different complementary therapies, it would be impossible to list every one available in this short chapter but you'll find a brief outline of the most popular ones below. Complementary therapies can have varying results for different people. Whether they really work or not the benefit of trying them is they are natural and chemical free and offer the body the best possible chance to heal itself. The effectiveness of various therapies largely depends on the skill and integrity of the practitioner. When choosing a therapist, make sure they are registered or accredited with the relevant governing body and go for personal recommendations when possible. Always seek the advice of your doctor for a proper diagnosis of the ailment then consult your own reference books or a registered practitioner and feel proud that you're doing the best you can for your family.

A rough guide to complementary therapies

Acupuncture
This originated from the Far East. Needles are inserted into the skin to rebalance the body's chi or energy. It can be used to treat numerous ailments.

Aromatherapy
The use of essential oils derived from plants and herbs to treat minor complaints and more serious illnesses, as well as being useful around the home, is commonly used. Oils can be burned in a diffuser, used

in bathwater, inhaled and used as massage oil. It's often handy to get yourself a small reference book for the basics, but if you're pregnant, make sure you consult a specialist for any specific problems. Oils should never be used neat on the skin with the exception of a spot of lavender for burns and tea tree for spots and pimples. If consulting a specialist, especially for a massage, try to avoid those based at spas and beauty salons. They tend to be more general and relaxation centred. Try to find a holistic specialist who knows how to treat everything from physical ailments to emotional problems.

Homeopathy

Based on the theory of similars stating that any substance which can make you ill can also be used to cure you if administered in a small enough dosage, homeopathy was discovered by a German doctor in 1790. Comprehensive homeopathy kits for travel, first aid, pregnancy and birth are available for home use from specialist suppliers, health food shops and some pharmacies. Remedies can also be bought individually. While home treatment can work, seeking the help of a qualified practitioner is recommended for more serious conditions as homeopathy requires some integrated and ongoing diagnosis.

Herbalism

We use this in our every day lives without us even realizing it: dock leaves for stinging nettle rash, parsley for smelly breath and echinacea for the immune system. Herbs used range from the exotic to the common hedgerow variety. Remedies can be taken in pill, tincture, cream or compress form and treatment is usually ongoing. Some herbal remedies are available in high street pharmacies. You may want to keep a stock of some of these in your green first aid box (see above).

Flower remedies

Developed by Doctor Edward Bach to treat emotional issues, essences of a plant are captured in water and bottled. This therapy is as yet unproven but these supposed remedies are so popular that they can often be purchased in local pharmacies. Rescue remedy is the most popular. Australian and Himalayan bush remedies and rainforest remedies are also available.

Cranial osteopathy or cranio-sacral therapy
This is a gentle manipulation of the bones especially the skull and spine. It aims to normalize the natural rhythms of the body, help circulate the blood and balance the lymphatic system. Children seem to be especially responsive to this and it's often used to treat babies who cry a lot, have problems sleeping or severe colic. For adults it's great for neck, back and shoulder pains, migraines and circulation.

Osteopathy
Developed in the 1870s by an American frontier physician, Andrew Taylor Still, this is a system of diagnosis and treatment, usually by manipulation, that mainly focuses on musculoskeletal problems (though a few schools claim benefits across a wider spectrum of disorders). Osteopathy differs from chiropractic in its underlying theory that it is impairment of blood supply and not nerve supply that leads to problems. Manipulation of muscles and joints are designed to reduce stiffness and tension, and to help the spine move more freely. Osteopathy can help treat conditions such as slipped disc, arthritis, lumbago, sciatica, neuritis, rheumatic aches and pains, tension headaches, postural defects, sports injuries, digestive disorders and menstrual pain.

Reiki
A form of Japanese spiritual healing, the practitioner acts as a channel for external energies which stimulate healing, placing their hands over parts of the body without actually touching it to channel the energy to the correct area. It's a subtle and relaxing therapy often useful for dealing with stress, headaches and emotional issues. Reiki is also useful during pregnancy and is a component of the Gentle Birth Programme. It can also be used to simulate labour. Again, there is no proof of its effectiveness, but if it feels good and works for you, why not?

Reflexology
This is a therapy that works with pressure points and energy zones on the feet and hands. These correspond to areas of the body. Applying pressure to these points triggers the body to

heal itself. A good therapist can diagnose problem areas and blockages within the body's energy flow just by feeling your hands and feet. Patients can normally feel when a problem area is found as the corresponding area on the hand or foot can be tender and even slightly painful. With some basic information you can easily treat young children at home. Like acupuncture, reflexology originated from the Far East.

Holistic health

This basically means approaching our health as a whole: mind, body and soul. Modern medicine often treats the symptom without looking at the root cause of an illness and treating that. It also assumes that our individual physiology is exactly the same but subtle differences in our environment, state of mind, diet, lifestyle and genetics can mean that we really need a treatment which deals with our ailment on a more personal level. The following factors also contribute to our personal health and well-being as a whole.

Stress

This is one of the major reasons for absence in the workplace, alongside colds and flu (which could be partly attributed to stress too). Worryingly, more and more children are suffering from stress. Our modern lifestyles tend to prevent us from taking things in our stride. We are constantly working against the clock even when we go on holiday, with two weeks to chill out then back to work. As parents it's important that we look after ourselves so that we are able to cope with the demands of family life. There are some really simple ways to help manage stress in our lives such as taking some time out each day to be completely quiet and alone, exercise and fresh air, homemade massages from a partner or friend, bathing, reading, hobbies and counting to ten! These are simple but so many of us find it hard to incorporate these small changes into our lives. For more serious symptoms of stress there are several more intensive practices like deep breathing techniques and yoga. Homeopathy, herbalism and aromatherapy can also be used to deal with stress.

Exercise

This is an integral part of a healthy lifestyle. With an increasing amount of people in sedentary jobs sitting on our bums all day and the advent of DVDs and computer games, we're becoming overweight, depressed and ill. More children in developed countries are now overweight than ever before and can be prone to type-2 diabetes, heart disease and bullying. Going to the gym is a good start but exercise that doesn't involve TVs, loud music and gets you outdoors is far better for your soul. Gyms are also pretty pricey. Swimming, cycling, yoga (for kids too), running, sports, walking and dance are all excellent forms of exercise and some of them are even free!

Fresh food

Packed with naturally occurring chemicals in the form of vitamins, minerals, proteins, enzymes and acids, fresh food not only keeps us fit and healthy but can also be used to cure illness. For example, celery is supposed to be good for respiratory ailments, chilli for inflammation, garlic for natural immunity and fertility, radish for coughs and sore throats and pineapple juice for digestion and cardiovascular diseases. Carrot is a good all rounder and has recently been found to contain a chemical which can help prevent cancerous tumours. Food has been used for centuries for its curative properties and there's no reason why we can't still use food wisely in conjunction with a healthy lifestyle, complimentary therapies and modern medicine when required. A burger in a bun just won't cut it! For more information about the medicinal properties of fresh foods see the Taking it further section.

Sleep

Sleep is an integral part of keeping healthy for adults and children alike, a lack of it can cause a whole list of health problems including irritability, a poor immune system, hyperactivity, depression, headaches, and the list goes on! Make sure you and your children get as much sleep as possible and when older babies fall into a routine, try to stick with it. Most of us experience sleeplessness or insomnia at some stage in our hectic lives. Clearing the mind of worries or problems by thinking them through before lying down in bed helps clear the mind. Reading a little before bed can also help. Bedrooms should be as quiet and dark as possible with all electrical equipment switched off at the socket. For some people, children and adults alike, relaxation tapes help. Bananas and warm drinks (not caffeine or alcohol based ones) such as chamomile and barley-based drinks aid sleep. The herbal remedies valerian and passiflora may be used to help insomnia.

Green parenting guide to health

🌿 Eat healthily, get as much sleep as possible and exercise regularly. Avoid processed foods and eat as many fresh foods as possible. Only use antibiotics and medicines when absolutely necessary. Use the odd home remedy such as honey and lemon drinks.

🌿🌿 Adopt a healthy lifestyle and attitude. Invest in some basic guides to food and everyday natural remedies and use these when possible. Try to use GPs for diagnosis, then do what you can yourself to treat ailments as naturally as possible. Consider vaccinating children carefully before making a decision. When resorting to modern medicines, use sparingly and purchase from small local pharmacies rather than from large chains or supermarkets. This helps support local business.

🌿🌿🌿 Keep a green first aid box. Find some reliable complementary therapists that suit your needs and stick with them for the treatment of family ailments. Gather as much information as you possibly can for self-diagnosis and treatment of the more basic ailments. Consider regular therapy sessions as a form of prevention. Treat family health as a holistic practice incorporating mind, body and soul!

8

Clothes and accessories

In this chapter you will learn:
- *how to avoid unnecessary chemicals in clothes*
- *how to buy green clothes and accessories cheaply*
- *how to prioritize your needs.*

There's no getting away from it. We live in a consumer-led society. We believe that we are defined by our possessions and how we look. Our culture, society and politics are also defined by what we consume or purchase. Some people even believe that what we choose to buy has more political clout than how we vote. No matter where you stand, part of being a green parent involves making sure that we use our money to consume as responsibly as possible. Remember, every little helps and how you spend your money contributes toward the big global picture. If consumers show a preference towards more ethically or sustainably produced goods it forces larger global corporations to follow suit and change their practices.

Clothes

Clothes are a necessity but we rarely question the processes they go through before we put them on and we're all too quick to dispose of an item because it's so last year. Cotton is the most widely used resource for the production of clothes but it uses more of the world's deadly pesticides and precious water supplies per kilo than any other crop. Six pints of water are needed to produce one bud of cotton and children as young as seven are used as cheap or unpaid labour in the cotton fields. Cotton is treated with up to 25 per cent of the available pesticides for crop production, a highly toxic cocktail that is released into our waterways and is responsible for over one million agricultural deaths in the developing world per year according to the Pesticide Action Network. These pesticide residues remain in the finished fabric. Conventional cotton production is also responsible for huge greenhouse gas emissions.

When fabrics have finally been produced they are then finished with a variety of dyes and chemicals designed to make clothing softer, wrinkle-free, fire-retardant, moth-repellent and stain-resistant (hence the prompt on the label to wash before first use). These chemicals have been linked with respiratory and allergic problems in children and adults alike and include:

- *formaldehyde products, often applied to prevent shrinkage*
- *petrochemical dyes, used to colour some fabrics, pollute waterways as well as remaining in the fabric*
- *Volatile Organic Compounds (VOCs) and dioxin-producing bleach*
- *nylon and polyester are made from petrochemicals, whose production creates nitrous oxide, a greenhouse gas that's 310 times more potent than carbon dioxide*
- *rayon is made from wood pulp that has been treated with chemicals, including caustic soda and sulphuric acid*
- *dye fixatives used in fabrics often come from heavy metals and pollute water systems*
- *acrylic fabrics are polycrylonitriles, which may be carcinogenic*
- *clothing and fabric that is treated with flame-retardant chemicals, such as children's pyjamas, emit formaldehyde gas.*

Mass-made clothes are often produced in cut and sew factories in developing countries which offer substandard working conditions and poor pay. A pair of brand name trainers costs more than the monthly wage of the average factory worker in India, who are often children less than nine years of age.

Buy organic cotton where possible, even if it's just the odd T-shirt.

You may have heard about the controversy over certain high street fashion chains and supermarkets being caught out over their factory workers' pay and conditions. When we buy that cute baby dress at a bargain price from our local supermarket, we may be buying into a lot more than we realize. If you'd like to avoid buying in and selling out to the big supermarkets and trendy high street stores read on. It's your cash and you're the boss when it comes to what you spend it on!

MATERNITY CLOTHES

Expectant mums may find that they are struggling to fit into their normal clothes within the first three months of pregnancy which can be tricky as a lot of maternity clothes are made for the second trimester. It's a good idea for would-be mums to invest in a few stretchy items of clothing if they're trying to conceive, as these pieces should take them through the first trimester and beyond. Sometimes buying a larger size of clothing can also work.

It's also possible to alter waistbands by hand or buy a waistband extender to insert in between zips. Try inserting contrasting thin triangular panels into the sides of existing tops for a funky bespoke new look.

The other issue is that traditionally, maternity clothes are boring, frumpy and can make the wearer feel about as sexy as a sack of potatoes. However, things have moved on and there are now many maternity ranges in both designer and high street stores that offer funky maternity options.

Save money by shopping in charity shops, online swap and sell, maternity exchange shops and local mother and baby sales such as those held by the National Childbirth Trust. Details of these are usually posted in local community centres and doctors' surgeries as well as on their website. Don't forget to ask friends and family for their hand-me-downs, but if you really want to treat yourself or you've got a special occasion to go to, there are now many local and national companies that offer lovely maternity lines which are made from organically produced materials or are fairly traded. Many of these can be found online, which is great for heavily pregnant mums who don't want to haul their heavy bump around the shops! With careful purchasing and ingenuity mums can save money and look lovely during their pregnancy.

BABY CLOTHES

No matter how you dress your baby, in the most expensive designer gear or just a nappy and a pair of wellington boots, he'll always be beautiful. The most important thing is that your baby is warm, dry, comfortable and protected in the most natural way possible. Newborns can be dressed in the same clothes for day and night and will grow out of them very quickly so you only need a small selection to see them through the first few months. All-in-one baby suits are probably the most versatile pieces of clothing and numerous companies now supply organic, fairly traded versions. The following tips should help you clothe your baby with minimum impact on your pocket and the environment!

Fabrics to avoid
Do not buy acrylic, polyester, rayon, acetate, triacetate, nylon, anything labelled static-resistant, wrinkle-resistant, permanent-press, no-iron, stain-proof or moth-repellent.

Natural fabrics
Try to stick to cotton, linen, wool, silk, hemp and cashmere. They tend to breathe better than synthetic fibres and naturally wick moisture away from the body as well as containing fewer of the chemicals found in synthetic fabrics. However, they will still contain pesticide residues and other chemical finishes so try to buy organic where possible. Many people also believe that buying silk is unethical due to the use of silk worms and the high input required.

Wash new clothes
Washing removes any synthetic chemical finishes used on the fabric. It's a good idea to sleep with a few of the clothes you intend to put on your baby when he is born so that your familiar smell is impregnated in the fabric rather than any perfume or chemical smell.

Organically produced clothing
This is less likely to contain as many chemical residues as conventional clothing, ensuring that your baby's delicate skin is kept as pure as possible. This is especially good for babies who may have respiratory or allergy problems. Organic production will also have less impact on natural resources and the environment. Many people see organic clothing as an expensive luxury item. However, organic clothing costs the same as high street baby clothes and is much cheaper than designer gear.

Fairly traded clothing
Buying these clothes ensures that the people who helped produce them got a fair wage and fair working conditions. By purchasing fair trade clothes you are doing your bit to ensure the equal distribution of wealth and making sure young children were not involved in the production of your baby's clothes.

Second-hand or charity shop clothing
This is a great way to be charitable without putting any money in a little white envelope every month. Your baby can have the benefit of clothes which have all the chemicals washed out of them and you have the knowledge that you've just helped a charity. Try visiting charity shops in the more expensive areas of your town. You can pick up really good quality clothes at rock bottom prices. Also, try local nearly new baby sales and don't forget to ask friends and family for hand-me-downs!

Locally or nationally produced clothes
They are generally of better quality than mass-produced ones and by purchasing these you are helping to finance a small cottage industry or company in your own country. This is an important

way to support your local and national economy and at the same time ensure that your product did not originate in a sweat shop.

Supermarket clothes
They may be cheap, but are inevitably mass-produced in a factory in a developing country (check the label). They will also have been treated with a cocktail of chemicals and are often contained in a mountain of unnecessary packaging. Not good!

Check credentials
If you'd like to limit your purchasing to companies which don't exploit poorer countries or the environment, you can check their credentials using publications such as The Good Shopping Guide and online websites such as Ethical Consumer and Sweat Shop Watch (see Taking it further for more details).

Choose clothes with nickel free fasteners
Nickel is a metal found in many everyday items from coins to jewellery and also the fastening in baby's clothes. Allergic reactions to nickel are very common, with nickel allergy being one of the ten most common causes of contact dermatitis. Symptoms may include swelling, itchy and red skin mostly located in the area of contact. Nickel allergy can affect people of all ages, but a baby's delicate skin may be particularly vulnerable. Most responsible baby wear manufacturers state whether the fastening on their baby clothes are nickel free or not. If it's not mentioned, chances are they're not nickel free.

Homemade clothes
These are the ultimate green option especially if you buy organic or fairly traded fabric which is easily available online. Simple pieces such as baby trousers and pinafores are pretty easy to make.

Prioritize needs by only buying key organic pieces
If cost is an issue try a mixture of buying second-hand, borrowing from friends and buying organic key pieces which will be in close proximity to your baby's skin such as sleepwear and underwear.

Naked is best
Going without clothes is not necessarily best for parents but definitely for babies. There's nothing they love more than the freedom to roam around without the restriction of clothes or a nappy!

OLDER KIDS AND THE REST OF THE FAMILY

Try to stick to your principles when it comes to dressing older children and the rest of the family too. Only buy what your really need and if cash is an issue, prioritize needs, buy second-hand and if you're buying new, try opting for fair trade or organic items. Many of these are made by small cottage industries and there is an ever increasing selection of really trendy ethical clothing to be found on the Internet. Many high street brands are now realizing that the market is changing and also supply an organic or fairly traded clothing line. If you feel particularly passionate about this issue there are a number of other things you can do:

▶ *Don't buy from any country with a poor human rights record such as China or Burma.*
▶ *Lobby your local MP to take action.*
▶ *Lobby high street brands to take responsibility by complying with the ethical training initiative labour codes and using organically produced fabric. Consider buying even one share in a company to entitle you to attend their AGM; its a great forum for having your say.*
▶ *Join a campaign to end sweat shop labour such as No Sweat or the Environmental Justice Foundation.*
▶ *Ethical and fair trade school uniforms are now being introduced in some schools and some companies are now set up to provide these as well as campaigning for ethically led purchasing of uniforms in all schools (See the Taking it further section for more details).*
▶ *Shop for jute or Hessian, as 4.5 million people in some of the poorest parts of the world are supported by the jute industry.*
▶ *Buy green or vegetarian shoes.*

Accessories

During pregnancy, birth and the early years of a child's life parents are bombarded by numerous adverts and sneaky marketing campaigns by big companies all designed to make you feel that if you don't part with your hard earned cash and buy the latest parenting gizmos and accessories you're not the best parent you could be. Your child may get burned, drown, have a bumpy ride, not be safe during a car crash and might even get bored! The list of marketing threats is endlessly exhausting and the good news is that it's also a load of rubbish. Save loads of money by not listening to the hype and listening to your own real, not perceived, needs. Your child needs you to protect him, keep him warm, feed him, keep him clean and love him. Having a three-way trendy travel system with designer interior print that turns into a small yacht for children of three years and above and a talking potty will not make a child a better person or make him safer or make him love you more, that's a fact.

Furthermore, the amount of resources, including labour (some of which will inevitably be from developing countries) used to make this product and ship it to your country for your needs over the next three years is huge and unnecessary. Consuming in this way simply isn't sustainable. So here are a few tips to help you provide your child with everything he needs whilst feeling satisfied that you've made your own informed decisions about what you need and that you've also done your bit for the environment your child will grow and thrive in.

PRAMS AND BUGGIES

These can be one of the most expensive items you can buy for a baby and they come in an unbelievable array of designs. If you'd like to save some money go for a design that will take you right through from birth to toddler. These kinds of prams are sometimes called pramettes. They basically convert from a pram to a buggy as your child grows. They are also lightweight and compact for getting on and off public transport and putting in cars. They come with all the luxuries of a normal pram and many also come with an integrated, easily detachable car seat. It might not be the all terrain three-wheeled trend machine you'd always dreamed of, but teamed with a good sling it should see parents and baby happily through until baby transport is no longer required! To save even more money try buying second-hand from charity shops or online and ask around for hand-me-downs. When buying second-hand always check brakes, safety mechanisms (including harnesses) and wheels are all in good working order.

MOSES BASKETS AND CRIBS

These look really pretty but are an unnecessary expense as your baby will have grown too big for it within three months. However, if you must have one, try to get your hands on a second-hand one. Babies will sleep pretty soundly anywhere that is safe and warm. If you have a breastfeeding cushion and a lambskin (a great investment for letting baby sleep and play on, buy an organic one if possible), make a little nest for her on the floor with these. Alternatively, buy a pop-up baby crib. This is an excellent idea for use in the house with the added benefit of being a handy sleep solution if staying away from home. It packs up very small so you can keep it for the next one! If you absolutely must have a new crib or Moses basket, look out for the eco-crib. It's cheap, funky and made of sturdy cardboard which can be recycled and packs flat for storage or travel. Alternatively, try looking for cribs and Moses baskets in ethical baby shops which often sell fair trade and natural material models.

COTS AND BEDDING

These can also be an expensive business but again, try to buy second-hand or ask around to borrow from friends and family. You may want to buy a new mattress though. This is recommended by health professionals. If you can afford it, buy organic or at least a natural fibre mattress. These are made of 100 per cent natural fibres such as wool, cotton, rubber latex, coir and mohair and are now available from many high street retailers. This ensures that your baby isn't sleeping next to the residues of chemicals with which conventional mattress are treated. Get more value out of your cot by buying one that converts to a bed and try to make sure it's made from wood sourced from renewable forests. Many green retailers also sell cots which haven't been treated with chemicals and have been seasoned using natural oils. They're also hand crafted, therefore an expensive option. You should also make sure that the cot you choose has a removable side so that it can be placed right next to your bed if you decide to co-sleep.

When prioritizing your needs, invest more in anything that comes into direct contact with your baby's skin, for example, mattresses, toiletries, underwear, nappies and of course bedding. Two sheets and a blanket should see you through. Try to make sure they're organic and cotton or wool and if you can get hold of some second-hand ones, even better!

BABY MONITORS

These are really only necessary if you live in a huge house – a baby's cry can measure up to 115 decibels, louder than a truck – or if your baby is vulnerable or has a medical condition. If you use a sling and let your baby sleep in the living room during the day and co-sleep at night you shouldn't really need one anyway, but if you do this is definitely something to try picking up second-hand.

BABY BIKE SEATS

These are a great investment and should last your baby for about three years. Getting out and about on your bike with your baby is the greenest way to travel, it's fun and it keeps you fit. Try to pick one up second-hand, but make sure you check that all fastenings and harnesses are working properly.

SECOND-HAND PURCHASES

These can give you a great buzz as you know that saving that extra bit of cash is going toward the family holiday fund or the 'I need a massage' fund, but you also get the satisfaction of knowing that you and your family are doing their bit for the environment by recycling! Charity shops, National Childbirth Trust sales, nearly-new sales, online second-hand marts and swap and sell forums run by many parenting sites such as BabyGROE are great resources for pre-loved purchases! So many baby things are only used for a few months, it seems crazy to buy them new.

GREEN COMPANIES

They are becoming more and more popular and are springing up all over the place, especially on the web. Whilst their goods may be a little pricier, saving money by only buying what you really need will make the odd purchase from them more affordable.

CONVENTIONAL COMPANIES

Check out their credentials if you have to buy something new, such as a pram or car seat. You can find out more about companies' ethical credentials on the Internet through various websites such as the Ethical Company Organisation, Ethiscore and Gooshing Company Ethics. Alternatively, buy a copy of the Good Shopping Guide (available from all good bookshops) which lists worldwide companies and rates their ethical credentials. See the Taking it further section for listings.

We need to establish sustainable consumption as the norm, balancing an acceptable quality of life with reductions in the amount of materials and energy we use. We need to make fashion sustainable and sustainability fashionable. It might seem hard to live with the changes required but it will be a whole lot harder to live in a world irreversibly damaged and impoverished by the environmental injuries of our current consumption. What a legacy to leave our kids!

Green parent guide to clothes and accessories

🍃 Prioritize your needs. Think about what your baby really needs. Buy second-hand where possible or borrow from friends and family. Use any money saved to buy organic, chemical-free essentials like bedding, sleepwear and underwear. Ask friends and family to get you fairly traded or organic baby goods as presents for your newborn.

🍃🍃 Avoid supermarket purchases and high street stores with a known reputation for unethical employment practices. Buy second hand and organic, fairly traded goods where possible from ethical parenting shops. Try to buy as locally as possible or at least goods produced in your own country.

🍃🍃🍃 Try to make do with what you've got by updating and adapting clothes you already have or try making your own. Buy second-hand but if you have to buy new, shop organic, fair trade and local. Extend your ethical purchasing to accessories, shoes and school uniforms. Lobby the corporate baddies to change their practices and hassle your local and national politicians too. Try to spread as much of this good practice to yourself and the rest of your family.

9

Play and education

In this chapter you will learn:
- *how to maximize your baby's development through play at each stage of its development for the first year*
- *how to choose green toys*
- *how to raise your children with green understanding*
- *how to get the best from mainstream education and the alternatives.*

Play and education go hand in hand, not just in the early years but also into the early teens. The old-fashioned ideas of the austere classroom and the 'children should be seen and not heard' attitude have been replaced with a more holistic attitude to teaching both in the nursery and the classroom, with more emphasis on social interaction and our environment. However, we may still have some way to go as most state systems of learning are still based on conformity and competition.

In our consumer-led society children are faced with a plethora of toys, games, bleeps, buzzes, colours and brands, with many five year olds being some of the most discerning consumers. Television has to be one of the biggest perpetrators of kiddie marketing and many specialists believe that the over-stimulation of our children's minds through television, computer games and high-tech toys is leading to a nation of lazy brained children and young adults!

Play and development

Babies start learning from the minute they are born and will become increasingly engaged with what is happening around them. Life is one big adventure which parents can have the pleasure of sharing with their children. Babies need their parents to create a secure environment in which they can explore their senses and discover light, touch, sound, texture, and taste. They also need help with new challenges and exploring their ever expanding world through active play.

Every child is different and will reach developmental milestones in their own time. However, different elements such as environment, personality, culture, heredity and a parent's involvement all have their part to play in the progress of a child's development.

THE FIRST EIGHT WEEKS

Babies are busy adapting to life outside the womb and forming attachments with their parents. Babies need lots of body contact during this time. As confidence builds so will more interactive and engaging behaviour, as well as those first smiles. A baby's hearing becomes highly sensitive and the eyes begin to focus effectively. However, even before focus is established babies still fix their gaze on their carer as if for reassurance. As coordination improves, babies will start to experiment with their vocal cords. At this age babies are fascinated by human faces, bold patterns and moving objects. Help stimulate your baby's ability to follow objects with a rattle or squeaky toy and use soft soothing sounds when communicating. A black and white mobile is a good toy as young babies like the strong, bold designs. Try giving your young baby clean, safe objects to feel and grasp.

When your baby can lie on her belly and push herself up, try placing a toy in front of her to catch her interest. Vary the way you hold her to encourage muscle development and talk softly and sing to her while you do this. Try laying your baby on different soft textures too.

THREE TO FOUR MONTHS

Babies become much more sociable and can easily identify people they see regularly, especially parents. Smiles of love and noises of contentment are now definitely for you. Laughing and crying to indicate what she likes and wants now make it easier for you to understand her needs. Her focus and senses are now much better developed, so it's a good time to start carrying your baby facing out towards the world in her sling so she can have a good look around. Babies at this stage can now babble and enjoy lots of stimulating chattering from anyone who'll oblige!

Babies at this stage have also learned to grasp things and like to hold and shake toys. They also like noises and toys which have a good texture for chewing and touching. Baby gyms are a great and simple investment at this age as they like to grasp and kick whilst lying down. Try to find a wooden or fabric version. When your baby is lying on her tummy try putting a ball just out of reach to encourage reaching, stretching and rolling over. Babies who can hold their head up whilst lying on their tummy are often ready to try short stints of sitting and standing supported by an adult.

FIFTH AND SIXTH MONTHS

Babies are learning to sit up unsupported. They have also learned that when things or people disappear or go away, it's not necessarily permanent. They are much more expressive both facially and in their body language and are fascinated by dropping objects. Every possible object is explored using the mouth! Words such as 'mama' and 'dada' are possibly now used but as yet, without meaning. Babies at this stage may be interested in solid food and enjoy exploring the texture with their hands. Babies also try to roll over at this age and some manage to push themselves up onto their hands and knees as practice for crawling. Placing a toy just out of reach may encourage this.

Babies love knocking down and grasping building blocks and will go for any hard objects they can find to chew on. They love games like peek-a-boo and hide and seek which help to reinforce that when things disappear, it's not always permanent. Babies also love repetitive nursery rhymes at this age. Toys with rattles, squeaks and bells are very good for babies of five to six months, as are nesting, sorting, posting and stacking toys. Baby will love pots, pans and wooden spoons and will enjoy playing on their own with a variety of toys and objects around them. This is a great way to encourage hands on play which facilitates the development of motor skills.

Babies also love playing in the bath at this stage, a bath seat which offers safety and support being a good second-hand buy. Mealtimes should be messy playtimes too when your baby is allowed to experiment with texture, colours and tastes. Many babies like a bit of gentle rough and tumble and enjoy being turned upside down.

CRAWLING BABIES

They are much more aware of the differences between themselves and others. They'll spend much of their time on the move, exploring their environment and for this reason it's a good time to make sure your home is baby-proof. Keep a watchful eye on your intrepid explorer! Strong affectionate bonds are formed with other important people in a baby's life and she'll play beside but not with other children. Communication consists of raising arms to be lifted, turning around when her name is called, remembering simple words and requests and beginning to recognize and assimilate a meaning to the word 'no'.

It's a good time to start naming things, as concentration on objects is now very intense. Babies begin to imitate sounds and will listen carefully to everything said to them. Speaking slowly and carefully helps babies to associate sounds with meanings. Your baby will really enjoy the sound of her own voice right now. Motor skills are well developed and some babies exhibit this by developing their own way of getting around such as bum shuffling rather than crawling.

This is a great time to introduce simple picture books made of tough cardboard or cloth. Continue to encourage crawling and movement by putting a toy just out of reach and place your hand against her feet so she has something to push against when she starts crawling. All the toys and games from five to six months are still popular as are toys with mirrors. Babies often try to pull themselves up to a standing position using furniture to balance against. Try giving your baby a toy to hold in one hand to encourage balance. Continue to offer support in standing positions. Baby will also enjoy being held and whizzed through the air as though flying, shoulder rides and dangling by hands, hips, etc.

THE END OF THE FIRST YEAR

Many babies begin walking and talking. Vision is almost fully developed and babies at this stage love to throw, drop and pull objects. Encourage your child's development by accepting a level of chaos in the house! Babies are totally engaged with everything going on around them and they become increasingly independent at this stage which can alternate with clinginess. Communication is much easier now as your baby will have learned to point to what she wants. Basic first words and eating and drinking alone also happen now. Babies at this stage can squat, cruise and climb.

Supporting babies by their hands while they take small steps is great practice for independent walking and babies love it. Attention spans are short so plenty of new stimulation in the form of big balls, spoons and drums is great. Take apart and put together toys are also popular now. Push along toys help develop walking skills. A wooden push along wagon with a hand rail is better for safety and development than bouncers or baby walkers as babies can go at their own pace and rest when they need to.

Make sure you read plenty of books with your baby at this stage and let her make her first scribbles with some non-toxic crayons. Create tunnels and shapes to crawl in and through using cardboard boxes, blankets and chairs and allow your baby to play outside with a basin of water, some pots, cups and spoons or a shallow swimming pool in warm weather but never leave baby unattended around water. Make sure you respond to any games your baby initiates.

Toys

We've all seen it: baby gets new toy, baby shows little interest for toy and much more for the box. There's a good reason for this. As a baby develops her world becomes an increasingly interesting place and too many over-complicated toys just become a distraction to learning rather than an aid. In our culture we tend to over-stimulate children with a plethora of unnecessary toys. Babies soon get bored with too many toys and will ignore them. Many toys are mass-produced for large corporate toy companies in factories in developing countries. Similar to the mass production of clothes, many of these factories have come under question for their worker rights and conditions. You can check many toy companies' ethical credentials on the Internet through various websites such as the Ethical Company Organisation, Ethiscore and Gooshing Company Ethics. Alternatively, buy a copy of the Good Shopping Guide (available from all good bookshops) which lists worldwide companies and rates their ethical credentials.

Toys that bleep, buzz (i.e. contain batteries), are rubbery and brightly coloured, are a distraction to practical learning from a baby's immediate environment. They also carry hazards such as phthalates or plastic softeners used in soft PVC toys, synthetic furs, fibres, dyes and electromagnetic fields from battery-powered toys, not to mention the environmental impact of producing packaging and transporting these toys around the world and their eventual demise to the local landfill site!

Phthalates have been used in children's toys and other household goods for the last 50 years but questions over the effect of the chemicals when ingested into the human body (they are known to be reproductive toxicants, disrupting hormones and damaging reproductive organs) led to some forms of phthalate being banned by the EU for use in children's toys and feeding accessories. Some companies now label goods as phthalate-free. However, there is still no overall ban on the use of the phthalate group of chemicals and other countries don't have the same restrictions so toys and other household items made and imported from outside the EU may well still contain phthalates. Try to avoid plastic toys and if you do buy them, try to ensure they're phthalate-free.

Choose toys made of natural materials such as wood or fabric. Try to ensure that the wood used is made from sustainable forests and that material toys are ideally 100 per cent organic cotton. More and more companies are selling fair trade toys which ensure that the producer has been paid a fair wage and that no child labour has been used. Where possible, read labels to make sure they contain only natural dyes and varnishes. Select age- and skill-appropriate toys. Buy second-hand and swap toys with friends who have children too. Check out your local library to see if they run a toy library. You can hire out toys from here for a nominal fee and it's a great opportunity for parents and babies to socialize. Don't overload your child with toys. Choose a few carefully selected ones rather than lots of random ones and please don't forget to pass on your old toys to toy libraries and charity shops. Recycle, pass it on!

Alternative play options

Research has shown that toys don't have any educational value and can't teach cognitive or motor skills. They just encourage a child to practice them, just the same as the box the toy came in will.

A child's environment is one big educational toy! Electronic books which teach your child phonetics in a foreign accent don't really lend themselves to letting your kiddie smear it with food and then drop it down the toilet! Cramming a child's head with useful information in the name of early education is no substitute for quality time spent with her. She will learn, develop and bond with you rather than with the Disney character on the cute video. Here are some great activites and alternative play options for both parents and children.

SWIMMING

A great activity for young babies and older children alike, swimming promotes co-ordination, trust, muscle development, fitness and safety around water. Babies are born with a natural dive reflex which prevents them from inhaling under water. This ability lasts until about they are about four months old and is why babies are naturally confident in water. Introduce a very young baby to floating with you in a warm bath, letting her rest belly down on your chest with the rest of her body submerged. When you feel your baby is old enough and confident enough, introduce her to your local swimming pool and consider enrolling in a water baby programme. As children get older, build their confidence in water with regular visits to the local swimming pool or swimming classes.

WALKS

Walks with babies and older children alike allow a great opportunity to get some exercise and fresh air, chat and learn about the natural environment. Let older babies experiment with the texture of branches and leaves and stimulate older children's imaginations with stories about what might be living in the park, or take a plant identification book with you and set a goal of identifying five trees or plants correctly.

CARDBOARD BOXES

These can be adapted to be cars, play houses, shops, puppet theatres, space ships and just about anything else you can think of, as can a few chairs, sheets and clothes pegs. Children love to create, invent and make-believe. Once you have helped your child create her space let her decorate the box with crayons. If using old sheets and chairs, let her decorate them with tinsel, beads or sparkly paper.

COOKING

Doing this together is a great way to bond and to learn about where food comes from. It also helps introduce older children to the concepts of science, reading and arithmetic. Involve babies in cooking at a very early age by letting them play with pots, pans and wooden spoons while you are busy and as they get older you can introduce dried pasta and water to their play. Older kids will enjoy getting properly involved. Try letting them help with basic recipes and giving their creations away as presents. They'll be so proud! Alternatively, let your child bake their own play dough using a cup of flour, a cup of water, half a cup of salt, a tablespoon of oil and a tablespoon of cream of tartar. Blend together in a pan over a low to medium heat and allow to cool before letting your kids create.

HELPING OUT AROUND THE HOUSE

Let your children help with everyday tasks. It is a great way of helping them learn not only about their environment but also about collective responsibility and being part of a family unit. Older babies are perfectly capable of helping to tidy up by putting things in the bin or back in the toy box. They also enjoy playing with the water in the sink as you are washing the dishes.
It might be messy but it's a great investment for the future!
Older toddlers can help out with the recycling. This establishes good understanding and habits for the future. Kids love to hear the crash as the bottles drop into the bin as well as sorting out the different kinds of recycling. Remember to supervise kids when dealing with glass and metal. Older children soon become accustomed to being a productive and active part of the family if patterns are set early on.

MAKING STUFF

Creating anything from mobiles made of old CDs to a cloth book made of material scraps, is a great way to spend time with your child. If you're short on ideas try looking for an activity book at your local library or book shop or search the net for creative ideas.

A BUSY BOX

This is simply a cardboard box filled with every day bits and bobs for your child to explore. It can be adapted to suit your child's age and can contain everything from egg boxes and cotton reels to plastic bottles filled with pasta or lentils, with the cap firmly screwed on of course! Use your imagination, but make sure that the contents are suitable for your child's age and small items which could cause choking or sharp edges and ties are removed. As kids get older, the busy box can become the dressing up box.

SINGING, RHYMES AND PEEK-A-BOO

To enrich your baby's life and stimulate the development of speech, experiment with different sounds and types of music to see which your child prefers. Don't make the mistake of thinking you have to stick to music made especially for children and toddlers. This type of music is often pretty tuneless and created by a computer rather than real instruments. Children have a very discerning ear when it comes to sound so don't limit your child to 'the wheels on the bus'! Try joining a music group with your child or buy basic musical instruments to experiment with at home.

FAMILY NIGHT OR DAY

Spending time together as a family group is really important, so try to set aside some time each week for this purpose. Try games, storytelling, putting on a show or having film night and accompany it with some special food like homemade cookies, popcorn or cocoa. Sunday is often a good day for this as it's a time when every one is winding down and relaxed. It is a good start to the week.

GET INTO THE GARDEN

There's lots to learn and do in the garden, as well as great opportunities to get covered in dirt. Set aside an area for your child and grow some vegetables there together. Start with basic vegetables that don't need much attention such as pumpkins, or sweetcorn. These look really impressive when fully grown. Nasturtium, rocket, strawberries, beans, peas, tomatoes and herbs can be grown and eaten straight from the plant. These plants can also be grown in containers if space is an issue. Start a wildlife garden, you can buy packets of ready prepared mixed wildflower and grass seeds at any garden centre. These are great for encouraging a variety of butterflies, birds and insects to come into your garden. Let your child choose and plant a tree and let her watch it grow over the years. This is a great way to help a child understand time and the changing seasons. If you have space, try making a small pond, a great way to attract frogs and newts to your garden. Create a habitat pile with garden trimmings and windfall to encourage hibernating animals to your garden and try putting up bird and bat houses and bird feeders. Invest in a bird identification book and a pair of binoculars and do some bird spotting. Kids also love plants that smell good such as jasmine or magnolia and bushes such as buddleia help to attract lots of butterflies. Borrow gardening books for children from the library for even more inspiration.

If you don't have a garden, you could try finding out through your local council if there is any allotment space in your area. Alternatively, try growing herbs or salad vegetables such as rocket in window boxes. Fruit bushes, peas and tomatoes grow well in planters, while tomatoes, peppers and herbs can be grown indoors on a window sill.

PLAY GAMES

Babies and older children like to play both indoors and out. If there's a communal area where local kids get together to play make sure you get your child acquainted with it. Physical exercise is a great way to stimulate development and alertness which video games and television will never ever be able to replace.

KEEP PRODUCTIVE PETS

If you have a large garden get some chickens, ducks, geese or goats. Not only do they teach children about responsibility and the cycle of life but they also produce food in return for a vegetarian, low calorie diet! And of course you can eat them if you're not vegetarian and are so inclined! Keeping chickens is a lot easier than you might think. You can now buy chicken homes together with food, chicken and instructions from several eco-companies, many of which can be found on the Internet.

Social life

In more traditional cultures, babies are cared for by a wide, extended social group of family and friends. This provides babies with several different people and other children to interact with as well as providing a much needed break for the baby's mother or main carer. We humans are extremely sociable creatures and this is one of the major ways in which we develop emotionally and intellectually. However, in our society with our nuclear families and demanding jobs it's not uncommon for a baby to spend all day, every day with one carer and to have no more than a few other people in their everyday life. This can be a lonely and exhausting experience for all parties involved!

Make sure that both you and your baby get out and about and socialize as much as possible with family and friends. If you don't have many in your area try joining parent and child classes or groups, visiting baby friendly cafes, soft play centres and toy libraries to meet other parents and their children. You'll enjoy the adult company and your baby will really enjoy and benefit from the interaction with other babies.

Television

As well as being the culprit for aiming powerful marketing and advertising campaigns at children, television also encourages conformity and a lack of independent thought, kills creativity and disrupts concentration. As children who watch more than one hour of television per day become more passive, so their active imagination diminishes and opportunities for active play with others decreases. They have shorter attention spans due to the influence of rapidly changing images and sounds. They come to expect this and become bored if they are not stimulated in this way all the time. This can lead to frustration and behavioural issues.

Completely eliminating television from your family's life may not be an option, but cutting down on the amount of time the television is used makes it a treat rather than an every day part of life. Children that are accustomed to occasional TV watching tend to get bored with it after about half an hour as they are used to more active play. Cutting down on TV time creates more time for interaction between the family which leads to better relationships. Without the powerful advertising on TV our needs tend to be more real than perceived. It is easy to be sucked in, especially for children. Limiting TV time also gives you and your family the chance to be more creative, to read more books and listen to the radio. There are lots of great radio productions for children and adults alike. Ditching the TV completely will not only save on license fees but also satellite and digital viewing fees.

If you do have a television, limit viewing time to a maximum of one hour per day and cover it up when not in use. Make it a treat by having a family film night as previously mentioned and experiment by having a TV free holiday or a month without TV. When you do watch television, try to watch quality programmes such as natural history, plays and dance or watch a channel that doesn't have advertising.

Education

For many adults, school is remembered as a place of large grey buildings, badly coloured walls, horrible toilets, school yard bullying, conformity, boredom and dodgy school dinners. In a post war era there was a need for mass education, conformity and a frugal supply of material and food, but society has moved on from this era and the education we offer to our children should reflect this. In many ways there have been great improvements, but the average school experience remains centred on regulations the confinement of four walls, tests, exams, conformity and often poor nutrition. Although the situation is improving, too many children receive no physical education after the age of ten years and children as young as five years old now sit compulsory tests.

Imagine a school class where the teacher walks in dressed as Henry VIII, takes the whole class outside and teaches them the history of this king's life by getting them to act out their own little part in history. Wouldn't that be a bit more interesting and exciting? This may sound completely unrealistic but many people are beginning to seek out and develop education that is more suitable to our modern world and initiated in this way. One of the most essential components of modern teaching is environmental education.

ENVIRONMENTAL EDUCATION

This has been thrown into the spotlight recently as our governments have decided to take the environment and the consequences of the pressure we are putting it under more seriously. It's really important that we take responsibility for our individual impact on our environment. A large part of this can be achieved by making our children aware of environmental damage and the steps we can take to prevent it. Children are naturally fascinated with the world around them which makes it extremely easy to engage them, no matter how young, in basic environmental education. This might all sound a bit heavy but that's only because it seems like a big lifestyle change to us adults because our governments have ignored it for so long it has become a crisis. In actual fact, it's just a natural evolutionary progression and a bit of a different way of thinking, teaching and being. For youngsters it's child's play!

Incorporating recycling, composting, gardening, nature walks and nesting and feeding places for wild animals and insects into everyday routines is a fun way to introduce basic environmental education. You can now buy many board and computer games designed to teach children about the environment, conservation and recycling. If your children do like to watch a bit of TV, encourage them to watch natural history programs. Encourage kids to conserve energy and water at home by teaching them to turn off taps when brushing their teeth, have showers instead of baths and only to flush the toilet for number twos. Teach them about switching off lights, putting on extra clothing when cold rather than the heating and avoiding battery-powered toys.

If you really want to get involved, join a conservation group and take part in their family activities and events. This is also a great opportunity to meet like-minded families.

Childcare

This is also a form of education. Choosing childcare can be influenced by many factors including work, cost, location, available funding and convenience. Some kinds of childcare are a little greener than others and each has its pros and cons. As a basic guideline, here are some of the options and issues you may want to take into consideration when making your choice.

CHILDMINDERS

Childminders offer flexible childcare which is more personal, and often based in a home environment. Childminding involves a small group of children but many may not offer the stimulation and educational play you'd like. Take time to find one that is sympathetic to your style of parenting. If you're using real nappies, make sure they're happy to go along with this and that they give kids healthy snacks and don't rely on TV for entertainment. Ensure that children get outdoors at least once a day for at least half an hour. Bear in mind that childminders don't have to follow any national curriculum for education. They also offer competitively priced childcare.

SMALL LOCAL NURSERIES

These deal with smaller groups of children but follow the national curriculum and many offer a set standard of nutrition and outdoor activities. They are also subject to regular statutory checks. Smaller nurseries offer more personal service to each child and outbreaks of pests and diseases such as head lice and e-coli are easier to control in small groups. Small nurseries, whilst following the national curriculum, may offer less institutionalized care but can be a little more expensive. Again, check their stance on the use of real nappies.

LARGE FRANCHISED NURSERIES

Generally the most impersonal and institutionalized childcare options, many offer part-funded places and regular routines with guarantees of outdoor activities and regular progress checks. Their early opening and late closing hours may be helpful for many working parents However, dealing with large numbers of children tends to mean that pests and diseases will have a fantastic opportunity to spread and large institutions can become over cautious and surgical about cleanliness as a result. Mass-market nurseries are definitively not a good idea for parents who wish their children to be treated as individuals and wish to avoid institutionalizing their children.

NANNIES OR AU PAIRS

Nannies and au pairs offer one to one care which can be tailored to suit the exact needs of parents. However, children may miss out on valuable social interaction with other children and become very attached to their carer, which can be difficult for both parents and children. They are expensive and are not subject to the rigorous checks which nurseries undergo.

STATE NURSERIES

They offer places from three years old onwards but are restricted to half day sessions only. They are often connected to the local primary school and offer a valuable stepping stone to school life. They follow the national curriculum and are therefore subject to the usual checks, but many smaller state nurseries are also quite forward-thinking and adopt a more creative and open approach to the care and education of their children. And the biggest bonus – it's free!

ACTIVITY CLUB OR WRAP AROUND CARE

This is competitively priced but competition for places may be high as there are not as many of these as there are nurseries. Many focus on outdoor activities and creativity as a form of learning and will collect and drop children off from school or other nurseries at designated times. Care offered tends to be more personal and many are more likely to deal with real nappies, but they usually only cater for older children.

ALTERNATIVES TO MAINSTREAM NURSERY

These are much the same as the alternatives for school, as are the pros and cons, so refer to the next section for tips.

Alternatives to mainstream education

These are becoming more widespread as more individuals are becoming aware of the need for a major change to mainstream education. Small alternative schools and alternative teaching methods are cropping up in many localities as a response to this need. It's worth checking out your local area to see what's available as many aren't widely publicized. The more established options are as follows.

HOME EDUCATION

The practice of children being taught by their parents at home rather than at school is becoming more popular worldwide. Some studies have shown that home educated children are usually more advanced socially and intellectually compared to mainstream school children. They receive much more one to one attention, offering more opportunities for freedom of expression and questioning. They also get to spend more time with children of all ages as well as adults. (Home educated children normally get together on a regular basis with parents, carers and other home educated children of lots of different ages in their community.)

Most home education is child-led so learning progresses at the child's own pace. Some families do choose to set up a school environment with a fixed timetable. Home education starts at birth as we support our children through exploration, learning about their environment and the development of skills. As the child gets older, parents can act as facilitators to learning rather than teachers. Some people choose to support their child's learning with the help of a set curriculum and method. The Internet is a good source for further information on the various types of home study curriculum that are available.

STEINER WALDORF EDUCATION

This is based on the teachings of an Austrian called Rudolph Steiner who believed that play and movement was central to child education. Steiner schools offer a homely environment using Steiner-based teaching materials and toys of natural materials and colours which encourage imaginative play. Teaching follows the Steiner philosophy that humans are connected with the natural rhythms of our world and its seasons. Timetables are led by seasonal change which is celebrated through song and natural routines, marking the passing of time. Formal education does not start until the age of seven and focuses on natural development, creativity and learning at a child's individual pace.

MONTESSORI EDUCATION

Dr Maria Montessori, Italy's first female doctor, started this form of education in the early years of the twentieth century. She helped to transform our understanding of the nature of childhood through her work and teaching methods for children with disabilities. When Montessori opened her first school in 1907, the results were so outstanding that it caused a lot of interest in Italy and elsewhere. She realized the importance of these results and formed the Montessori Movement. Her work became internationally renowned. Her influence is reflected not only through the work of Montessori teachers in thousands of Montessori provisions across the world, but also in the practices of nearly every school for children.

FOREST SCHOOLS

Based on an innovative educational approach to outdoor play and learning, the philosophy of Forest Schools is to encourage and inspire individuals of any age. Through positive experiences, and participation in engaging and motivating achievable tasks and activities in a woodland environment, children are encouraged to develop personal, social and emotional skills. It was originally a concept developed in Denmark for pre-school children (under seven years of age).

Getting the best out of mainstream education

Although alternatives to mainstream education may be the ideal for some of us, they are not always practical and are often too expensive for the average income. They may not suit some children. For example, a Steiner-based education may be too creative for children with more logical or scientific minds and some children may simply respond better to more structure and routine. Whilst offering other options for learning, alternatives may take children away from mainstream culture, making it difficult for them to integrate in the future, and perhaps finding such intergration hard to understand. If your child attends a state or mainstream school, make sure you get the most out of it by trying the following:

▶ Try to spend as much time as possible with your children at home using the suggestions for alternative play and education suggested in this chapter.
▶ Don't push your children to perform at school and play down the importance of all tests and exams; emphasize instead the enjoyment of learning at your child's own pace.
▶ Make sure you involve your child in plenty of outdoor activities and environmental education.
▶ Get involved with your child's school by joining the parent–teacher association and attending committee meetings.
▶ Make sure you are proactive at parent evenings and if you have suggestions or criticisms, speak out; it's the only way to affect change. If the school isn't listening, contact your local authority.
▶ If your child is struggling and seems stressed at school let them take some time out. Don't force them to attend as you may find there's more to the situation than you think or the routine may just be causing burn out.
▶ If you do allow time out at home make sure it's filled constructively, learning through helping around the house or studying at home with no TV or computer games.

Green parent guide to play and education

🍃 Spend one to one time with your child as often as possible. Get outdoors with your child as much as you can. Avoid plastic, electronic toys and buy second-hand or use a toy library where possible. Attend a class or get-together with parents and their kids on a regular basis. Limit the amount of TV time and computer games you allow your child. Be as involved as possible with your child's schooling and don't put too much pressure on them to achieve.

🍃🍃 Enjoy time to sing, do arts and crafts and play games with your child. Create a busy box and try to buy toys made of natural materials without harsh dyes or chemicals. Educate your child about the environment and energy saving from an early age and enjoy classes with your baby. Send older children to classes which encourage their creativity and socialization. Choose a nursery school which is sympathetic to your needs and doesn't have too many children. Match school with wrap around care or time at a Forest School and join the school committee or PTA.

🍃🍃🍃 Choose toys carefully and only buy fair trade, organic or second-hand toys. Nurture your child's development by spending as much time with her as possible. Do as many arts and crafts as possible with your child and make homemade toys using every day items. Spend lots of time in the garden, keeping chickens as pets and growing your own vegetables. Cook together as much as possible. Home educate or use alternative schooling.

10

The green house

In this chapter you will learn:
- *all about toxins around the house*
- *simple steps towards making your house more green*
- *how to make the most of your garden*
- *how to keep a green pet*
- *green building basics.*

Every day we surround ourselves with toxic chemicals. We eat them, we put them on ourselves and we breathe them in. Nobody really knows what the full-blown effects of a combination of these chemicals have on our body but we do know that the incidence of respiratory and allergy-related illness in the western world is on the increase and we also know what some of these chemicals, commonly found in our household environment, are toxic. So why are they used when there are other alternatives? One word explains it all: profit. As long as we consumers want these products in our home then companies will continue to produce them. Only by changing our consumer habits can we effect change in our environment, not only for ourselves but also for the future of our children.

Toxins in the house

DECORATING MATERIALS

These contain highly volatile chemicals. Modern paints can contain up to 50 per cent solvents and volatile organic compounds (VOCs).

These are emitted into the air during the lifetime of the paint and can irritate eyes, nose, throat and nervous system. Try to use natural paints with a plant or mineral base instead, especially in children's bedrooms. Some mainstream DIY stores now stock these types of paints, as do several online companies. Wood preservatives also contain chemicals that are an irritant to the nervous system, so when buying them make sure they have a boron base, a naturally occurring mineral which is less harmful. Wallpaper contains fungicides which can emit fumes that contribute to indoor air pollution.

SOFT FURNITURE AND MATTRESSES

These often contain flame retardants, which are also used in plastics and computers. They are supposed to prevent the spread of fire. They build up in the air because they don't biodegrade, so they contribute to indoor air pollution. Several of them are known hormone disrupters which can interfere with the thyroid hormone and contaminate breast milk. Some countries have banned them and major companies such as IKEA have stopped using them. Always check the label and ask the company for more information. Formaldehyde is used to glue wood, make insulating foam and preserve wood. It's used in paint, fabrics, cheap furniture and MDF. Inhalation can cause flu-like symptoms, rashes, cancer, inflamation of the joints and neurological illnesses.

Soft furnishings and bedding made of synthetic materials and non-organic cotton is full of irritating fibres and chemicals, as previously discussed in Chapter 8, so try to buy organic cotton, or hemp for soft furnishings and bedding. When purchasing mattresses make sure they haven't been treated with stain repellents and flame retardants. It's now possible to buy mattresses made of completely natural materials such as rubber, coir, wool and cotton which are completely untreated. These are quite expensive but a worthwhile investment for those with sensitivities and children. Buy pillows and duvets with natural fillings such as feathers or wool. These cost more but will last a lifetime and will keep you luxuriously snug and chemical free.

PVC DOUBLE GLAZING

This has a reputation for being the best energy-saving investment for draft-free windows but in actual fact it's not as efficient as wood. PVC produces a large amount of toxic waste in its production and if burnt in a household fire, emits hydrogen chloride gas, dioxins and phosgene leading to even greater risks from domestic fires. When disposed of, PVC emits toxic plasticizers and other heavy metals in landfill. The upshot is that it's pretty nasty, wasteful stuff so opt for wooden framed double glazing units instead!

WOOD

Wood is often finished with chemicals such as formaldehyde, especially chip board and MDF. Use softwood or European plywood instead and use conifer for kitchen worktops. When buying wood make sure it's sourced from sustainable plantations.

FLOOR COVERINGS

Most of these contain a cocktail of chemicals. Underlay and glue is required when carpeting, and the carpets themselves can release formaldehyde, a known carcinogen, for years. They are also a haven for dust, mites and fibres which can aggravate asthma. Vinyl flooring can contain phthalates, chlorinated paraffin or organotins which may cause various problems from liver, kidney and testicular damage to immune and nervous system problems and birth defects. Chlorinated paraffin is a known carcinogen. Choose alternative flooring such as wood, cork or ceramic tiles but make sure any glues, backing, underlays and varnishes used in the process are as chemical free as possible. Alternatively, use a completely natural floor covering such as coir or sisal, both of which are derived from natural fibres.

DAMP PROOFING TREATMENTS

These contain potentially carcinogenic chemicals which contractors go to great lengths to protect their workers from, so why would you want to have them injected into your home to remain there for as long as you do? Aside from any damage to the respiratory system, the damage to your wallet can also be extreme. Damp proofing is not a cheap treatment. Ask a specialist in old buildings or an eco-build advisor before embarking on any treatments. You may discover that inserting vents or fans into a room, clearing gutters and blockages, re-plastering or re-pointing a wall as well as keeping a good balance between heating and ventilation in your house can be enough to remedy the problem. If re-plastering or re-pointing try to use lime-based plaster or mortar instead of cement as it absorbs and releases moisture more readily. For damp problems on outside walls, try lowering the ground level alongside the offending wall by digging a trench approximately six to eight inches deep depending on the severity of the problem.

WOODWORM TREATMENTS

This is another costly chemical treatment that is over zealously recommended by most contactors. Only active infestations need treated. A simple way to test for this is to tape a sheet of paper over the infected area and leave it for a few weeks. If the worms are active, holes will appear in the paper. This could save you hundreds if not thousands of pounds and yet another chemical invasion in your house.

EMFs OR ELECTROMAGNETIC FREQUENCIES

These are emitted by all electric appliances and cables. There are suggestions that these can interfere with the natural energy flows within the human body causing stress, irritability and sleeplessness. To minimize the impact of EMFs in your home, especially bedrooms, minimize the amount of electrical appliances you have in each room especially televisions and computers. Switch everything off when not in use, especially monitors. Cover screens when they're not being used. Place crystals on or next to televisions and VDUs. Feng Shui experts believe that crystals can help dissipate EMFs. Liquid crystal screens emit less than the old fashioned cathode ray tube televisions and computer monitors so swap them if possible. You can also help neutralize the harmful effects of VDUs and electrical appliances by having lots of plants in your home. Cacti and peace lilies are especially effective. Place plants as close to the offending appliance as possible.

Plants are also an effective way to cleanse the air in your house. According to the ancient tradition of Feng Shui, they increase the oxygen content, improve the humidity and negative ionization within the home as well as lifting the energy within. The common spider plant is especially effective at removing formaldehyde from the air. Other plants which are effective at removing chemical residues from your environment, including formaldehyde, carbon monoxide and benzene, are bamboo palm, Chinese evergreen, weeping figs and mother-in-law's tongue. A couple of plants per average sized room should do the job.

INSULATION

This uses HCFCs which are a replacement for the CFCs responsible for helping to deplete the ozone layer. Unfortunately, HCFCs are not completely harmless either. Use cellulose, cork, wool or foamed glass as insulation alternatives.

WATER

Water is treated with chemicals which find their way back into our environment when we use it. Some of these chemicals may be harmful. Chlorine, for example, is commonly used in the water purification process. It is a bleaching agent that destroys proteins in hair and skin. This can cause dry hair and itchy skin. Filter out the chlorine in your household water by tapping into a local natural supply or fitting a household water filter.

The alternatives

DE-CLUTTER

Make your home feel brighter and airier. We all need to feel that our home belongs to us and is a calm refuge from the pressures of modern day living, but coming home to a dark house with junk everywhere can sometimes make us feel more stressed. Our personal environment can reflect our state of mind so clear the clutter, throw open the windows and let the light in!

ACCESSORIES, GADGETS AND APPLIANCES

Do we really need these things that fill most of our houses and occupy a great deal of our time, whether through entertaining us, or through their maintenance and cleaning requirements? The biggest green tip here is to cut down on these. The second option is to buy green, ethical or fair trade where possible. Many online companies and catalogues now offer a selection of household accessories and gadgets for the eco-conscious householder. You can buy everything from recycled glass crockery and plastic chairs to fairly traded, organic cushions and throws, energy-saving light bulbs and solar powered fountains! There are also several companies which offer alternative solar powered or wind-up gadgets such as radios and mobile phone chargers.

Buy second-hand energy rated appliances where possible and if buying new always make sure your product has the highest energy rating possible. If you'd like to take it even further check out the ethical credentials of electrical appliance companies before making a purchase and avoid those who have a bad ethical or environmental record. You can find this out on the Internet through various websites such as the Ethical Company Organisation, Ethiscore and Gooshing Company Ethics. Alternatively, buy a copy of the Good Shopping Guide (available from all good bookshops) which lists worldwide companies and rates their ethical credentials. See the Taking it further section for listings.

Here are some green household tips:

▶ *When considering DIY and renovations, first decide if you really need them. If you do, consider all the materials and techniques you will use and their implication on your environment.*

- Over 78 per cent of the world's original old growth forests have been logged or degraded, so make sure any wood or wooden furniture you buy is certified as sourced from sustainably managed forests.
- Recycle old curtains to make new ones or put them into a textile recycling bin.
- When renovating, try to use recycled materials such as tiles, baths, radiators and wood floors as this can be both a cheaper and more stylish option and well worth the effort – try local salvage yards and second-hand goods brokers for more information.
- Use local tradesmen who are sympathetic to more traditional methods of building.
- Rent or share power tools with neighbours or friends because most are made in developing countries as disposable objects therefore their short shelf life means that both you and the person who made it are getting a raw deal.
- Dispose of all paints and chemicals properly as around 20 to 30 per cent end up in our water courses which damages wildlife, the environment and in the end, costs the tax payer a lot of money to clean up.
- Take all paints and chemicals to a special disposal facility and recycle paint at your nearest paint recycling plant – ask your local authority for more details.
- Open windows every morning to get rid of the volatile organic compounds emitted by the electrical equipment in your home which can irritate respiratory systems.
- Let as much light as possible into your home and consider installing skylights or sun pipes into particularly dark areas.
- Invest in an ionizer to clean the air of dust, pollen fumes and dirt.
- Instead of normal wax candles, buy unscented beeswax candles which contain no chemicals and avoid scented candles as they can also emit chemical compounds into your home.
- If you really love scented candles, try adding a few drops of essential oil to a beeswax candle.
- Choose second-hand furniture or re-condition old furniture where possible.

- When revamping kitchens try to replace just the cupboard and drawer fronts rather than the whole carcass saving money, time and resources.
- Save money and resources by purchasing a vacuum cleaner that does not require a bag.
- Use reclaimed wood from local dumps and skips for DIY projects.

In the garden

As mentioned previously, gardening and growing your own vegetables is not only great exercise and an education in its own right, it also makes a small contribution to a wider local ecosystem.

FUEL-POWERED LAWN MOWERS

These produce as much pollution in one hour as 40 cars. Use an electric mower or better still use a manual one. Remember that lots of grass doesn't necessarily make for an interesting garden. Use garden space for wildlife meadows, rockeries, ponds, flowerbeds and vegetable patches.

HARSH CHEMICAL PESTICIDES

These are just another pollutant to our immediate environment and if used on fruit and vegetables, residues stay there for us to consume. There are numerous natural ways to deal with pests and diseases and lots of books written on the subject. Alternatively, check out the Soil Association website for some handy hints and tips.

CREOSOTE

This is a powerful irritant when inhaled and easily pollutes the garden when washed by rain into the soil. It has also been found to be carcinogenic. Since 30 June 2003, creosote has been withdrawn from sale to householders in the UK.

PEAT COMPOST

Peat, like coal, is a limited natural resource and a huge percentage of peat bogs have been damaged or destroyed. Peat bogs are important to conservation because they can teach us about both our past and future environments. Use peat-free compost and make sure the plants you buy aren't potted in peat either.

GADGETS

Avoid energy-hungry patio heaters, gas BBQs and wooden furniture sourced from tropical rainforests.

COMPOST

Almost one third of domestic household waste could be composted, but instead it goes straight to landfill where an absence of air and oxygen results in it taking a very long time to break down. Composting is easy and many local authorities now encourage it by offering free or very cheap composting bins and lots of advice. Simply pop all your uncooked kitchen leftovers such as peelings, eggshells, ground coffee and tea bags in the bin with garden waste such as grass, prunings, leaves, sawdust and weeds and let the insects and micro-organisms do their natural thing. All you need to do is turn it occasionally and in no time you'll have the most rich, free food for your garden possible and not a compost bag in site! You can also put cardboard in there to give it a bit of fibre and don't forget to throw some worms in too. If you really want to go for it, buy a food digester, available from most garden centres and DIY stores. They do much the same as a normal composter but you can also put cooked food in there!

HABITAT PILES

Create these with leaves, wind-fallen branches and prunings. These also encourage diversity and are a particular favourite of the hedgehog.

BAT, BUTTERFLY AND BIRD BOXES

As well as being a valuable safe haven for local wildlife, these will fascinate your children. Encourage birds into the boxes by popping in a piece of naturally moulted sheep wool.

LADYBIRDS

Encourage ladybirds as they eat greenfly. You can do this by buying a ladybird house for your garden which comes complete with ladybird larvae. The house provides a safe place for the ladybirds to grow and breed and they can eat up to 8,000 greenfly per day!

BUSHES AND PLANTS

Buy ones that are indigenous to your own country if possible, and go for plants such as fruit bushes and herbs, that not only look pretty but also produce something that can be eaten or is medicinal. If you're really clever you can grow plants together that actually benefit each other in some way, for example they could help pest control or create shade or other preferred soil conditions. This is a method of growing called permaculture. If you're really into your gardening why not get a few books out of the library or look online to find out more. Try to make your gardening minimum effort with maximum output for you and your family.

The green pet

Pets are loved by many families in the UK but can they be green? The worldwide pet care industry is worth an estimated US$27.5 billion and is predicted to rise to US$40 billion by the end of 2010. Unfortunately our love of pets doesn't leave the environment unscathed either. There is no doubt that keeping pets can have a valuable impact on family life and the emotional and educational development of children, but we have to ensure that we keep on considering the environment.

VEGETARIAN PETS

Try to stick to animals such as rabbits or guinea pigs. Better still keep vegetarian pets which produce something you can use, such as chickens, ducks or goats. If you have a dog try to feed him scraps instead of buying dog food, boost his protein intake with scraps from the butcher, or even try to make him vegetarian. If you feel that you have to buy food, purchase dry food in bulk as this uses less energy and transport.

RESCUE CENTRES

Look for your pet at a rescue centre or find one that needs re-homing. If you can't have a pet at home encourage older kids to volunteer at a rescue centre or sponsor an animal.

CATS

It is best to neuter cats. The number of abandoned cats is rising every year with thousands waiting to be re-homed.

Put a bell round your cat's neck. Domestic cats kill all sorts of local wildlife and can have a severe impact on its fragile balance. A bell can reduce predation by up to 35 per cent.

Buy a biodegradable cat litter made of recycled paper. This can be composted but the solid waste has to be removed first. Most pet stores and supermarkets now sell this kind of cat litter. This option is much better than putting non-degradable soiled litter into landfill sites.

BUY NATURAL

Don't buy your pet plastic toys. Try natural alternatives such as natural rubber, cloth or latex. Use homeopathic and natural remedies for your pets too. There's no difference between human and animal remedies so use the information in Chapter 7. You can get more advice from the association of homeopathic veterinary surgeons.

SCOOP YOUR DOG'S POOP

Dog faeces contains the minute eggs of roundworm which can live in the soil for up to two years. If ingested these hatch, then burrow through the gut wall damaging the liver and lungs. They can even cause blindness. Children playing in parks are most at risk so bag it and bin it!

COMMERCIAL FLEA SPRAYS

Don't use these, as they are designed to attack a flea's nervous system and can cause reproductive problems in pets so it's not really the kind of chemical you want around your children. Use a non-toxic flea collar instead. Try adding garlic pills or brewers' yeast, available from health food shops, to your animal's food to repel the fleas. Your pet exudes the odour through its skin which is repellent to them. Alternatively make a herbal flea collar. Visit the Pesticide Action Network website for more information.

RSPCA

Insure your pet with the RSPCA. Not only will you have the peace of mind knowing that you will be able to care for your pet should the worst happen but you'll also be donating 10 per cent of your premium to the RSPCA to help less fortunate animals.

The green build

If you really want to go for it why not think about throwing it all in, turning your back on the concrete jungle and building your own green house? Ideally the ultimate eco-house is carbon neutral, using power from a number of different green energy sources with non-polluting furnishing and fixtures, perfectly insulated with underfloor, self-regulating heating and windows which self-adjust to filter light and air as you need it. If the ideal ecotopian home isn't quite within your budget don't fret, many self-build homes come as state-of-the-art timber kits. They are cheaper than bricks and mortar, use one tenth of the amount of energy it takes to construct a conventional house and save money because they can be built in weeks rather than months. You can add to the kit with other eco-products such as roof tiles made of recycled materials and you can use rock foundations instead of cement.

Eco-houses can be made of a multitude of different mediums such as straw, rammed earth and wood. Many books, companies and Internet sites now offer information on eco-builds and renewable, earth-friendly building materials. If you're interested try visiting eco-builds in your area or eco-build shows. Don't forget that you can also employ environmentally conscious builders, thatchers, architects and wildlife consultants. Earth buildings reduce the impact on the landscape as well as saving between 30 and 60 per cent in energy costs. A straw bale house can last for up to 100 years, it looks beautiful and has excellent warmth and sound insulating properties as well as being a fraction of the cost of traditional buildings. For more details please see the Taking it further section.

If you are building a new home consult an expert in passive solar design and consider incorporating this into your new home. The heat of the sun can be used to heat your home, by placing double glazed units at optimum positions to maximize the warmth from the sun. This can be achieved at virtually no extra cost if installed whilst the building is being constructed.

Similarly, it's possible to incorporate building techniques into your design which maximize natural airflow and therefore act as a passive cooling system minimizing unnecessary energy use. Again, incorporating this during the construction stage of a house means that it can be done at almost no extra cost.

Improved acoustic and thermal insulation can also be achieved by the inclusion of a green roof. This is basically a roof with soil on top, where you can plant grass and wildflowers. As well as its energy conservation properties it looks lovely and provides an extra habitat for birds and wildlife.

Don't forget to team your build with renewable energy solutions, recycling options and ethical investments, mortgages and insurance (see the next three chapters).

Last but not least, there are an increasing number of eco-villages and environmentally conscious new builds springing up all over the place. Never ones to miss out on a slice of the pie, some mainstream house builders have even dipped their experimental big toe into the eco-housing market. These may come at a price premium and there may not be so much choice but if you've got the cash and you want minimum impact for minimum effort then these might just be for you!

Green parent guide to the green house

🍃 Make sure you let plenty of air and light into your house, especially in children's rooms. Use plenty of plants around your home to cleanse the air. Switch off all appliances when not in use. Try to buy only what you really need and buy second-hand furniture where possible. Try to avoid using carpets in your house and invest in some untreated natural cotton for your child's bedding. Use your garden as much as possible or grow some vegetables indoors. Make sure pets are neutered and all dog poop is disposed of properly.

🍃🍃 Try to carry out any renovations required as sympathetically as possible, avoiding unnecessary chemical treatments, and replace only what is necessary with reclaimed or natural materials if possible. Try to buy organic bedding and fair trade furnishings. Buy energy rated appliances and check credentials of companies before making a purchase. Limit the number of electrical appliances you have in your house. If you want a pet, try to obtain one from a rescue centre. Feed it scraps or dried food. Stick to vegetarian pets where possible. Install bat, bird or butterfly boxes in your garden and put aside an area for a vegetable and wildflower patch. Compost kitchen waste.

(Contd)

🍃🍃🍃 Build your own eco-home using natural resources. Reclaim as many building materials, fixtures and fittings as possible. Buy fair trade, organic, ethical and recycled furniture, accessories and soft furnishings. Use natural floor coverings such as sisal or coir. Install ionizers and water filters. Keep chickens and grow organic vegetables in your chemical-free garden using permaculture methods. Invest in a food digester.

Recycling

In this chapter you will learn:
* *why recycling matters*
* *how to recycle the easy way*
* *how to recycle particular items.*

Reducing how much rubbish we send to landfill is the main objective of recycling and should be a priority for everyone, not just those wanting to be a green parent. Recycling has already been mentioned frequently throughout this book. It doesn't just mean putting your bottles in the bottle bank, it also means reducing the amount you use and reusing items wherever possible. As a parent you will be seduced by more disposable items than ever before. Knowing how to dispose of them, reduce their environmental impact and pass this knowledge onto your children is one of the greenest parenting steps you can take. It doesn't matter how big or small your recycling effort is, just do it! Every little makes a difference.

Waste

For generations we have let local authorities take our waste away and dump it in very large holes in the ground called landfill sites. As our population rises and we consume more and more, an increasing amount of rubbish goes to our already bursting landfill sites, so now we're running out of space in which to dump our rubbish. As landfill space competes with housing developments (nobody wants to live next to a landfill site) the options for disposing of our masses of throwaway items and packaging are minimal. Incineration isn't really an option as incinerators like landfill sites emit toxic gases and ashes that need to be safely disposed of, usually in landfill sites. What is the solution? Producers could design more durable items but technology is moving at such a rate that many electrical goods are obsolete within a few years. Packaging could all be recyclable but it's easier and cheaper and glitzier to stick with the current over-packaging. So it's left to us, the consumers, to create the change by becoming more aware of what we buy, how much we buy and how we dispose of it. We must reduce, reuse and recycle!

Reduce, reuse, recycle

Many local authorities now have set state or government targets to reduce the amount of waste going to landfill sites so we'll probably all see changes in the way our rubbish is collected. This should make recycling a whole lot easier. But it's not all just specifically about recycling. We can also help reduce the amount of waste being taken to landfill sites by reducing and reusing.

REDUCE

Reduce what you send to landfill by buying less or buying second-hand. When you do have to buy a new item, try to buy quality goods which will last as long as possible and are easily repaired, maintained and upgraded. Buy products made in your own country or, better still, buy locally and support your local economy whilst cutting down on packaging and transport costs (energy and hard cash!). When you do have to go to the supermarket, take your own reusable shopping bags and avoid buying over-packaged goods. Buy at local shops rather than supermarkets, or at shops which offer a refill service for liquid products and dry goods to cut down on packaging. Try buying in bulk from a wholesaler or get together with friends to start a purchasing co-op. Avoid buying disposable items such as plastic razors, cameras, cups and plates, or nappies.

REUSE

Reuse old items where possible and think twice before throwing them in the bin. Instead of throwing furniture away give it a new lease of life by recovering, stripping and/or re-painting, re-varnishing or having it repaired. Look after things well instead of treating them as replaceable and when things do break don't throw them away unless they really can't be fixed. Find new uses for old items such as using old plastic bottles as cloches for seedlings. Donate things you don't want to charity shops and appeals or ask friends and give them away. Alternatively, put them on a swap site on the Internet site and exchange your unwanted items for something else you've always wanted! Of course you could always sell things at a car boot sale or on the Internet. Your rubbish might just be someone else's dream!

RECYCLE

This saves energy, natural resources and reduces waste disposal. Recycling one glass bottle saves enough energy to power a washing machine for ten minutes! Governments have now realized the importance of recycling and have made huge advances in the last few years, but we still have a long way to go. Make recycling easier for yourself by getting into the habit and organizing a good recycling system that works for your household size that even the kids can do! Be sure to give items a wash before recycling them as some items may be useless if dirty. Buy recycled items where possible. More and more eco-conscious companies are springing up which offer all sorts of goods made from recycled materials, such as lampshades, chairs and bookcases. Get into composting as it can remove up to two-thirds of our dustbin contents, much of which is paper and card.

Recycling rumours

In an attempt to dodge responsibility, companies and consumers alike often quote some recycling rumours to get them off the hook. Recycling is still in its infancy, with new uses for recycled items, different ways of recycling and new, more environmentally friendly recycling plants being developed to cope with the new demand. However, as with everything, we have to start somewhere. Here are a few rumours that shouldn't stop you!

It costs more to recycle things than to make new things

This is not true. Recycling saves on many costs such as water, energy, raw materials, dealing with the pollution caused by producing new goods and extracting the raw materials.

Transporting recyclable goods causes lots of pollution

It is true that currently there aren't enough processing plants to deal with demand, therefore many items have to travel long distances. However, as more uses are found for recycled materials and demands for them rise, the market will expand and more local processing will take place as a profitable and environmentally friendly solution. The upshot? Keep recycling. Your bottle makes a difference!

Recycled products are expensive or poor quality

Some recycled products can be more expensive than the general average, but more consumer demand for recycled products will bring the price down so keep on purchasing them. Recycled products are generally of higher quality (especially true of hand-crafted goods) and are sometimes, particularly in the case of aircraft tyres, used as a safer alternative to new products. Some materials can be recycled indefinitely without losing quality, such as aluminium, glass and some plastics. Others can be incorporated into other recycled materials to make completely different products.

Green glass just gets thrown away

Only contaminated glass gets thrown away. It is true, however, that we need to find some new and exciting uses for glass which would give the market a boost.

Recycling takes up too much time and space

Once you are into a routine, it'll take less time and become a habit rather than a chore. Some people think that they have to remove labels but in fact they don't need to be removed from bottles or tins. Recycling won't take up more space as your local authority will probably supply you with separate bins.

It is cheaper to throw things away than recycle

This is not true, as up until recently landfill costs have been heavily subsidized. As governments are starting to realize that the viability of landfill is now questionable, they have introduced landfill taxes which will steadily increase, making recycling an increasingly cheaper option.

Washing items for recycling uses more energy than is saved by recycling them

It doesn't if they are washed at the end of dish washing.

Commonly recycled items

These can be separated into 12 basic groups. The following are simple guidelines for each group.

PAPER AND CARDBOARD

	Reduce	Reuse	Recycle
Newspapers and magazines	Buy them less often.	Donate to waiting rooms.	Make paper logs for fires; kerbside collection; paper banks.
Writing paper	Buy recycled.	Use both sides.	Compost.
Telephone directories		Use to raise the height of computer monitors.	White ones can be collected kerbside or put into a paper recycling bank.

(Contd)

	Reduce	*Reuse*	*Recycle*
			Yellow ones to recycling centre or back to distributor; compost or shred for animal bedding.
Cards and postcards		Donate to charities who sell them on to collectors. Give them to schools or nurseries for art projects.	Hand into recycling points at shops. Check to see if your local authority will collect them with your cardboard.
Envelopes	Buy envelopes with cellulose windows which biodegrade.	Stick blank labels over the address and reuse.	Remove windows and compost or recycle with paper.
Drink cartons	Avoid where possible.	Use as plant pots (on their side for seedlings).	Buy pre-paid recycling labels for tetrapaks. Some local authorities now recycle cartons.
Egg boxes		Offer to children's groups/schools or farm gate shops.	Compost.
Catalogues			Recycle with newspapers and magazines.

	Reduce	*Reuse*	*Recycle*
Cardboard		Use in the garden as a weed suppressing mulch, then cover with compost.	Shred for animal bedding; compost; some local authorities also recycle cardboard.

METAL

	Reduce	*Reuse*	*Recycle*
Cans and tins		Can be made into pretty tea-light holders.	Rinse and recycle to can banks.
Scrap metal		Take to scrap metal dealer.	Take to recycling centre.
Kitchen foil	Use alternatives for wrapping food such as paper bags or greaseproof paper.	Clean, flatten and reuse. Some charities and appeals collect it.	Some kerbside schemes collect it but it is collected separately from tins and cans.

GLASS

	Reduce	*Reuse*	*Recycle*
Milk bottles		Return to supplier.	Plastic ones can be recycled in some areas. Recycle in plastics bank.
Bottles and jars	Buy refillable ones.	Use for all kinds of storage, food, screws and nails, paints, etc.	Remove lids and recycle them with tins and cans. Rinse jar and put in bottle bank or for kerbside collection.

(Contd)

	Reduce	*Reuse*	*Recycle*
Glasses			Never put broken glass in bottle bank. Wrap in newspaper and bin.
Light bulbs	Buy low-energy bulbs, especially for areas where lights are on for a long time.		Some groups now recycle light bulbs. Check local listings and the Internet for details.
Sheet glass		Cut to create smaller panes or use to make cloches for seedlings.	Take to household recycling centre or glass merchant.

PLASTIC

There are a mind-boggling array of different plastics that make their way in to the home each day in the form of packaging, carrier bags, bottles and packets. Unfortunately, their period of usefulness is often short-lived and many of them are simply discarded into household waste and ultimately landfill. The recycling of plastic does require effort but ensures that these energy-filled resources that would otherwise lie unaltered in the earth can be recycled with relative ease over and over again.

In order for the maximum gain to be made it is important to separate the plastics into their different families before taking them for recycling. This doesn't have to be a chore, in fact it can be made into a learning activity for children and adults alike. Most plastic materials will carry an abbreviated code name and a code number to make it easy for the keen recycler:

1 *or PET – Polyethylene Terephthalate, e.g. water bottles*
2 *or HDPE – High Density Polyethylene, e.g. milk bottles*

3   *or PVC – Polyvinyl Chloride, e.g. detergent bottles, food wrap, blister packaging*
4   *or LDPE – Low Density Polyethylene, e.g. plastic bags, bin liners*
5   *or PP – Polypropylene, e.g. margarine tubs, some carpets*
6   *or PS – Polystyrene, e.g. some yoghurt tubs, foam packaging, meat trays*
7   *other – Polycarbonate, acrylic, ABS*

Facilities to recycle types 1 and 2 are usually found in supermarket car parks as well as at municipal recycling centres. Others can be more difficult to recycle but don't be put off; a small family can quickly become avid plastics recyclers by simply filling a bag with empty milk and juice bottles.

LDPE is one of the most prevalent plastics in the weekly shop as it is what our shopping is often carried home in. An easy way to lessen this burden on the environment is to reuse existing bags or, even better, invest in tough, reusable ones. Bags made of recycled tyres or reclaimed polypropylene aren't hard to find.

TEXTILES

	Reduce	Reuse	Recycle
Clothing	Simple question: do I *really* need a new shirt?	Donate unwanted items to charity or hand children's garments on to smaller kids. Some supermarket car parks and authorities have clothes banks.	Clothes can be recycled to make items such as insulation or mattress filling and cloths.
Shoes	A new sole can revitalize an otherwise worn out pair.	Again, charity shops will take shoes in a usable condition. Some supermarket car parks and authorities have shoe banks.	

(Contd)

	Reduce	*Reuse*	*Recycle*
Curtains		The Curtain Exchange will find a new home for your drapes rather than see them go to waste. www.thecurtainexchange.net	As for clothing.
Rags and off-cuts		Why buy cloths for dirty work when old towels and shirts do the same job?	
Bedding		Old sheets and duvet covers make ideal dust sheets for decorating.	Natural materials can be composted, but it is best if they are shredded first.
Carpets	Carpets can be rejuvenated by a good deep clean.		Man-made fibres in carpets are usually polypropylene. Check locally for facilities for disposal.

CHEMICALS

	Reduce	*Reuse*	*Recycle*
Pesticides	Avoidance is the best policy, as nature has always managed quite well. Natural alternatives are readily available.		Never put them in the drain – contact local authorities for disposal details.

	Reduce	*Reuse*	*Recycle*
Photographic chemicals			Gone digital? Film contains silver which can be reclaimed, ask in a photographic shop for details of how and where to donate.
Engine oil			All municipal recycling centres will have facilities to dispose of oil as it is highly illegal to put it down the drain!
Paint	Avoid toxic paints, particularly the ones containing and marked VOC.		Check with local charities for where your old paint can be donated to be used by those who are more needy than you. www. communityrepaint. org.uk
Batteries	Wind-up watches/toys need only finger power.	Use rechargeable batteries. Avoid battery-operated equipment.	Many local authority recycling centres will take car batteries for recycling. Some companies take their old batteries back.
Aerosols	Pump sprays use no greenhouse gases as a propellant.		Check with local authority for recycling facilities.
Anti-freeze	Avoid where possible.		If you can't use it up give it to someone who can.

FOOD

	Reduce	Reuse	Recycle
Cooking oil		Can be used to make bio-diesel. National and local schemes are available on the Internet.	Can be composted but works best if mixed with fibrous materials first.
Cooked food	Make meals from leftovers. Store foods correctly for maximum lifespan.	Stale bread can be made into croutons, breadcrumbs or bread and butter pudding.	Uncooked vegetables can be composted and food digesters are available for everything else.

WOOD

	Reduce	Reuse	Recycle
Prunings		Create a habitat pile in your garden.	Perfect for the compost bin.
Timber			All recycling centres will welcome your off-cuts, otherwise use the energy to heat your house in a wood burning stove.
Sawdust		Use in pets' cages or keep some to soak up oily messes in the garage.	

	Reduce	Reuse	Recycle
Ash		Use around the plants in the garden as a form of potash.	Compostable in small quantities.

CERAMIC

	Reduce	Reuse	Recycle
China		Can be used in mosaic work.	Don't include it with glass recycling – it contaminates the batch.

SOILS

	Reduce	Reuse	Recycle
Peat	Avoid if possible as peat bogs are being destroyed at an alarming rate. Homemade compost is a much better option.		
Grow bags			Add leftovers to the compost bin.

PLANTS

	Reduce	Reuse	Recycle
Grass cuttings	Lawns don't always have to be perfectly trimmed!		Composts well when aerated with other materials.

ELECTRICAL APPLIANCES

	Reduce	Reuse	Recycle
Fridges and freezers	Buy the best energy rated appliances in the first place whenever possible.	Buy second-hand reconditioned appliances.	These really must be disposed of at recycling centres where their harmful components such as CFCs can be assessed and handled accordingly.
Computers		Outdated hardware for you may be extremely useful to someone else and many charities will ensure all data is removed before reconditioning.	

RECYCLING MORE UNUSUAL ITEMS

Wellies
Cut them down to make pool shoes.

Single-use cameras
If you can't go digital be sure to have the exposures developed by a firm who have a sound policy of recycling.

Water
Divert waste water from the home for use in the garden.

Tyres
Specific companies make a variety of products as diverse as mouse mats, children's playground surfacing and anti-fatigue matting.

Ink cartridges
These can often go back to the manufacturer, otherwise many charities such as Oxfam have programmes in place to reduce waste.

Tools
These can be sold directly or donated to local charities who will distribute.

Radiators
These are valuable scrap metal; take to a recycling centre or scrap merchant.

Mobile phones
Can be returned to supplier or to many organizations (such as Tesco) who will arrange reconditioning and reuse.

Spectacles
Most major opticians will have a process for donated glasses to be reused in developing countries.

Medicines
These should be returned to the chemists for disposal.

Lino
Real lino can be shredded and recycled by composting; synthetic versions can't.

Corks
Corks can be composted or used for kids' arts and crafts.

RECYCLING TIPS

In the future we may not talk about waste as a problem but rather as a valuable resource. Zero Waste is a philosophy for the twenty-first century which maximizes recycling, minimizes waste, reduces consumption and ensures that products are made to be repaired, reused or recycled to nature or the market place. New Zealand and Australia both have whole designated districts and states committed to a Zero Waste philosophy. Britain has one Zero Waste zone and the US has led the way with an Urban Waste Park in California as an alternative to a landfill site, which is committed to repairing, reusing and recycling everything!

Things are progressing slowly but in the meantime, do your bit. Try looking at the contents of your bin and sorting it into recycling categories. You'll be surprised at how little is left! If we stop and think about where it's all come from and where it's all going we can begin to make more educated choices for ourselves and our families. Involve the whole family and have fun as you all enjoy the satisfaction of knowing you're doing your bit for the environment. Here are some handy tips to help you on the road to the three Rs:

▶ *Get informed by buying a household recycling book and contacting your local authority to find out exactly what they can recycle and about any other useful recycling centres in your area.*
▶ *Mark junk mail 'Return to Sender' and post it back or register with a mailing preference service.*
▶ *Use plastic storage boxes or store things in a bowl with a plate over the top rather than using plastic bags and food wrappings such as tin foil and cling film.*
▶ *Send electronic cards by email rather than paper cards where possible.*
▶ *Use cloth hankies instead of paper tissues.*
▶ *Don't burn rubbish on outdoor fires.*
▶ *Buy a paper shredder.*
▶ *Volunteer at a local recycling programme.*
▶ *Get involved with schools, local authorities, recycling organizations and help spread the message.*
▶ *Start your own resource recycling centre.*
▶ *Take part in a master composter programme.*
▶ *Kids' packed lunches are a major source of unwanted packaging so try to make most of it at home avoiding*

ready-made sandwiches and snacks, and by putting your own mixes and juices in reusable containers.

▶ *Children are great recycling assistants, as not only do they love sorting through the rubbish but they're also pretty good at recycling containers, material, wool, string, and paper by making them into unique works of art.*

The green parent guide to recycling

🍃 Try to reduce how much you consume. Reuse your own bags when going shopping. Recycle paper, glass and plastic where possible. Don't replace things unless you really need to.

🍃🍃 Recycle as many items as possible and start composting. Avoid buying disposable items. Register with a mailing preference service. Involve and educate the kids about recycling. Let children create pieces of art from used items. Cut down on packaging in your kid's lunch box.

🍃🍃🍃 Buy recycled products where possible. Do a composting course. Get involved with recycling organizations and help spread the message. Aim for Zero Waste!

12

Energy

In this chapter you will learn:
- *why saving energy is important*
- *how to save energy in your house*
- *all about carbon emissions*
- *about renewable energy solutions.*

As natural energy resources such as oil, coal and gas become more and more scarce and energy prices soar, governments are gradually beginning to take the idea of renewable or green energy much more seriously whilst still considering the nuclear power option. Not only are our natural energy resources declining but our insatiable desire to power and light everything we possibly can – electricity demands are expected to rise by 15 per cent in the next 15 years – is also creating carbon (CO_2) emissions which contribute to the greenhouse effect and its associated problems of climate change. Some governments are so worried that they have actually introduced targets for individual household energy production with incentives of grants and installation help for householders. This is called a microgeneration strategy. Homes and businesses would produce green energy for their own use and sell the excess back to the national power grid. The aim of this is to cut both fuel bills and CO_2 emissions. We have a long way to go until every household can independently produce its own energy, but what can families and parents do in the meantime?

Household energy-saving tips

The first step to saving energy around the house is being conscious of how much energy you are wasting. Start with the basics such as switching off lights and appliances when not in use and making sure your house is draft proof by shutting curtains when the sun goes down, fitting draft excluders round windows and doors and making sure lofts and pipes are properly insulated (40 per cent of heat loss in a typical home is through the walls and the loft!).

If you're cold get the family to put on an extra layer of clothing rather than turning the heating up (this could save you up to 10 per cent on your annual heating bill too.) Fit energy-saving light bulbs. They last 12 times longer than normal ones and again save you cash.

Insight

Ensure you always have a full load in your washing machine and wash at 30 degrees celsius as often as possible only using a 60 degree programme once in a while when, for example, the nappies need a bit of a cleaning boost.

WATER

There are many ways of saving resources here:

▶ *Fit a water meter to monitor your household's usage – some local authorities will fit and supply free of charge.*
▶ *Teach kids to turn off taps when brushing teeth.*
▶ *Turn taps off when shaving.*
▶ *Fix leaky taps.*
▶ *Encourage the family to shower rather than have baths.*
▶ *Collect rainwater and recycle for watering the garden, as the global drinking water shortage isn't helped by quenching the thirst of a garden with valuable drinking water.*
▶ *The average household flushes 50 litres of water down the toilet per day, so teach your kids the 'if it's yellow let it*

mellow' mantra and don't let the kids flush the loo unless it's a number two!

▶ *Fit a water-saving device, such as the Hippo Water Saver, into your toilet cistern – saving up to 3 litres of water per flush.*

GAS

If you are buying a gas oven, make sure you get one with electric ignition. A gas pilot light constantly burns gas.

HEAT

Follow these heat-saving tips:

▶ *If you're going away for more than a day be sure to switch off your heating system.*
▶ *Keep south-facing windows clean to maximize heat generated by sunlight.*
▶ *Programme central heating to go off when you're asleep and use extra covers to keep you warm at night.*
▶ *Only heat rooms being used.*
▶ *Block up unused chimneys and close fireplace dampers when fire is not in use.*
▶ *Regularly bleed radiators.*
▶ *Buy sustainably produced local charcoal.*
▶ *When replacing a boiler or water heater, ensure it's the most energy-efficient model.*
▶ *Maintain the efficiency of boilers or water heaters by having them regularly maintained.*
▶ *Install double glazing if you can afford it, but if not use plastic secondary glazing.*

Insight

Put radiator foil behind each radiator to reflect heat back into the room.

ELECTRICITY

Follow these electricity-saving tips:

- ▶ *Only fill the kettle with the amount of water you really need or invest in an eco kettle.*
- ▶ *Defrost fridges regularly to stop them having to work harder and use more energy.*
- ▶ *Allow food to cool before putting it in the fridge.*
- ▶ *Use a low-heat programme in dishwashers and try to avoid using the drying and rinse hold programmes, only switching it on when it's completely full.*
- ▶ *Wash all clothes on as cool a washing cycle as possible (see water section earlier).*
- ▶ *Avoid using a tumble dryer and if you really have to, make sure the clothes are well wrung or spun first and clean the lint tray, as clogged ones cause the machine to use more energy.*
- ▶ *Steam irons use an extra 1,000 watts per hour more than non-steam irons, so don't buy one, but if you already have one, ditch the steam and use a water spray instead.*
- ▶ *Don't leave appliances with remote controls on stand-by, as it's estimated that US households waste $5 billion worth of electricity per year by doing this and worldwide between 5 and 15 per cent of household energy consumption is wasted.*
- ▶ *Turn off chargers and adapters when not in use.*
- ▶ *Don't leave outside lights on.*
- ▶ *Make sure all electric appliances you buy are the most energy-efficient models.*

COOKING

Follow these easy energy-saving tips:

- ▶ *Cover pans with lids when boiling water and it will boil 6 per cent faster. Turn down the heat once it has reached boiling point, then after a bit turn it off and the vegetables or eggs will continue to cook and will be warm for serving.*

- *Make sure pans are on the right sized ring and if using a gas cooker don't let the gas lick the sides of the pan as this means it's up too high and you're wasting gas.*
- *If boiling vegetables or rice, boil more than you need and use later.*
- *If roasting meat, make the most of having the cooker on and roast some vegetables too.*
- *Opening the oven door loses 20 per cent of the heat every time, so keep it shut if possible.*
- *Turn off the oven ten minutes before the food is due to be cooked and the remaining heat will finish the job.*
- *Defrost food properly before cooking to reduce cooking time.*
- *Switch to a green energy supplier which produces energy from renewable sources, causing less impact upon the environment.*
- *Choose a green tariff – the electricity supply company must obtain an amount equal to the total amount of electricity you consume from existing renewable energy sources – so that correspondingly fewer units of electricity will be produced in a power station from fossil fuels: there will be no change in the way electricity is supplied to your property and prices will be roughly equal and in some cases cheaper.*

If you're a new green parent the energy tips listed above will probably be enough to get you started. Don't forget to involve your children, as it's a learning curve for you all! If you've got the cash and are a real greenie then one or more of the options below might just be for you.

Carbon offsets

Carbon offsets enable people and organizations to reduce their carbon footprint therefore allowing carbon dioxide, one of the main greenhouse gases, to be either taken out of the atmosphere or reduced in another part of the world.

A carbon footprint is a measure of the impact human activities have on the environment in terms of the amount of greenhouse gases produced. It is measured in units of carbon dioxide.

There are a few ways of offsetting your carbon footprint:

▶ *Plant a tree to breathe in carbon dioxide and breathe out oxygen.*
▶ *Invest or donate to companies or organizations who are researching and developing renewable and sustainable technologies.*
▶ *You can buy energy-efficient technologies and donate them to developing countries.*

_____

Renewable energy for the home

There are now many grants available for making your own power at home but the initial cost can be unrealistic for most average income households. Although these options can help make substantial saving on energy bills in the long term, it would take most households years to recoup the initial outlay from savings made on lower energy bills. Some of these costs could be recouped by selling back excess power to the National Grid, but connecting back to the grid isn't available everywhere yet. So if you're considering kitting your home out to produce your own energy make sure you're fully committed and have done your sums.

CURRENT OPTIONS

The following are the current green energy options available for domestic use. Green technology is advancing at an incredible rate so it's worth contacting a specialist company in your area for more specific advice. Some useful contacts are listed in the Taking it further section at the back of this book.

Biomass heating
It uses wood chips in stoves or boilers connected to central heating systems.

Solar water heating systems
Under optimum working conditions they can provide enough hot water to meet half of a household's needs as well as make savings.

Photovoltaic (PV) systems
They convert the sun's radiation into electricity and promoters say they can cut as much as 50 per cent off electricity bills.

Micro-combined heat and power units
These operate like conventional hot water boilers but use excess heat to generate electricity for home use and they can also help save money on bills.

Ground source heat pumps
These pumps transfer energy from the ground into a long fluid-filled pipe buried under the garden which is then used to make hot water and underfloor heating, providing up to 80 per cent of a household's hot water and heating needs.

Domestic wind turbines
There are claims that these are able to provide up to 35 per cent of the average homes electricity needs, but planning permission is required to install them.

Grey water recycling systems
These collect waste water used for washing and recycle it for things such as the flushing of toilets, but for private domestic use these more technical solutions are not always the best solution on either financial or environmental grounds, as a small rainwater recycling system may, for example, have a larger environmental impact (materials, energy use for pumps, energy use by technician to maintain it) than the water use it is saving.

Rainwater recycling schemes
Rainwater gathered from the roof is used to help flush toilets and for other household uses.

The green parent guide to energy

🌿 Draft proof as many parts of your home as possible. Switch things off when they're not being used. Fit as many energy-saving light bulbs as you can.

🌿🌿 Remember that water is also an energy source. Save and conserve where possible. Maintain heating systems and appliances around the home so that they're running efficiently. Turn your heating down by two degrees. Save energy where possible and teach your kids to do the same. Switch to a green energy supplier. Make sure all appliances you buy have the highest energy rating.

🌿🌿🌿 Use energy-saving devices around the home such as eco-kettles and wind-up appliances. Install some renewable energy technologies into your home. Become involved in energy awareness campaigns in your area.

13

Holidays and travel

In this chapter you will learn:
- *what impact our travel and holiday choices have on our environment and others*
- *how to have a cheap and convenient green holiday*
- *some green travel tips.*

Airport expansion, CO_2 emissions, archaeological damage, threats to world ecology, exploitation of cheap labour and unfair profit distribution within the holiday industry have all led to the argument that the only truly green holiday maker is one who stays at home. However, the tourist industry provides income, jobs, and foreign exchange to communities and countries that really need them. Sometimes the money that tourists bring can be used for good causes such as the establishment of national parks. In many cases, poorer countries simply wouldn't be able to afford to create national parks without the money tourism brings.

Everyone needs a break, especially if you've got children, so completely eliminating travel is simply not feasible for most, but cutting down on how often we travel and how we do it can make a positive impact on our environment and the countries we visit. Here are some everyday things you and your family can do to make a difference.

Holidays

For some of the world's best responsible and eco-tourism holidays from tour companies and hotels with responsible travel companies, check out www.greenglobe21.com.

As little as 20 per cent of the cost of a package holiday may actually find its way into the local economy of the country of destination. The rest is lost to air fares, travel agents, hotel chains and imported food and drink. Holiday in your own country as much as possible. There are now more and more holiday guides designed to make holidaying in our own countries a voyage of environmental discovery, beauty and adventure. Many are much more family friendly too. Check the Internet for details of specialist companies.

CURRENT OPTIONS

Green Globe sign
This certifies hotels, airlines and travel agents that meet the World Travel and Tourism Council's standards for responsible and sustainable development of world tourism. Try to use travel companies that offer environmentally friendly holidays. They are now easy to find on the Internet and specialize in reducing the environmental impact of tourism.

Hostelling and camping
Holidays in your own country are a great, cheap, fun and green holiday option for families. Join historical societies and hostelling associations for discounts on accommodation and entry to historic buildings and gardens.

Organic holidays
There are more and more organically led hotels, B&Bs and guest houses all over the world that specialize in not only organic food but also minimizing their impact on the environment and protecting the local economy and traditions. Most of these are

also extremely family friendly. Visit www.organic-holidays.com for listings.

Small local tour operators
Deal with a specific place or type of holiday rather than the big mass-market operators.

Volunteering or working holiday
Some of these are designed to accommodate kids too. Half of your holiday is spent volunteering and half relaxing. You are guaranteed to experience a lot more local culture this way and it's a great way for children to make new friends and learn about how children from other parts of the world live.

House swap
Swapping your house for a few weeks with another family on the other side of the world means that you have all the comforts of home and are completely bypassing the tour operator with only flights or travel to arrange. Locals can also give you the best information about what to do in their area.

Written policies
Ask tour companies or hotels for their written policies regarding the environment and local people. If they don't have one, ask why not.

Hotels
Don't use free mini-toiletries; they are totally unnecessary and wasteful. When staying at hotels, reuse sheets and towels until they really are dirty rather than having them changed every day. This helps save on water, heat and detergent.

Travel
Walk, cycle or use public transport when on holiday.

Gifts
Try to buy locally made gifts or souvenirs and support local trade but avoid gifts made of products from endangered species such as ivory, coral, mahogany or teak.

Mosquitoes
Use mosquito nets rather than chemical or electrical mosquito repellents.

Sex trade
More than a million children aged 7 to 17 enter the sex trade each year and end up in brothels frequented by sex tourists. If you're on holiday and see anything suspicious don't turn a blind eye. Help to stop this sad trade by reporting anything suspicious to your hotel or the police.

Local culture
Respect local cultures by following and respecting their traditions but also by modifying your own behaviour, and use local guides.

Environment
Minimize your environmental impact while on holiday by avoiding the use of plastic bottles, wasting water, etc. Try to follow the same waste and energy-saving principles you would follow at home.

Travel

Transport is the most polluting element of most holidays because of the amount of CO_2 emissions produced, which contribute to the greenhouse effect and global warming. CO_2 is produced when fuel is burned. A return flight from London to New York produces more CO_2 per passenger than the average British motorist does in one year.

Scientists predict that air travel will be responsible for over half the annual depletion of the ozone layer by 2015. We can offset our personal emissions by planting trees to consume the CO_2 we've produced but it's not just our increased air travel due to cheap flights that's causing problems. Our increasing reliance on bigger, fuel-guzzling cars, sometimes more than one per household which we use to pop to the shops are leading to congestion, environmental pollution, increased respiratory illnesses, obesity and climate change.

Trams, steam-powered buses, inner city tuc-tucs, green taxis, community transport, hydrogen-powered cars and transport using bio-fuels are all currently being experimented with as a solution to our fuel and transport problems, but until these are widely available what can the average family do to create a brighter environmental future for their children and save fuel and money? Ditching our cars would be the greenest option, but let's face it, that's hardly what a working mum with three kids to transport to nursery school every day is likely to do. Here are some manageable steps that parents can take:

▶ *Don't use a car for a trip of a few hundred metres down the road for a bottle of milk.*
▶ *Try to use public transport where possible or if possible walk or hire a bike.*
▶ *If you have to travel to work by car see if you can set up a car share scheme.*
▶ *Drive more slowly, as a car travelling at 50 mph uses 30 per cent less fuel than one travelling at 70 mph.*
▶ *Turn car engines off if you're stopping for more than a minute.*
▶ *Try to walk the kids to school instead of using a car or use (or set up) a local walking or cycling to school scheme in your area, where trained parents collect children from their various homes and see them safely to school and back on a rota basis.*
▶ *Invest in a good hybrid style bicycle which will do for on and off-road use with a kiddie seat and good cycling helmets for both you and your child, making sure they're fitted properly and get out there and explore.*
▶ *Purchase bikes for older kids too and get them through their cycling proficiency course as soon as possible.*
▶ *Fit panniers or baskets to your bike and use it for going shopping too.*
▶ *Service cars regularly to ensure optimum running conditions.*
▶ *Don't buy big cars, buy the smallest to fit your needs.*

- *Fuel consumption can rise by one per cent for every 6PSI under the recommended tyre pressure, so pump up those tyres.*
- *Don't carry excess weight around in the boot of your car because it'll just cause your car to consume more fuel.*
- *If your car runs on petrol consider switching to an alternative fuel which will emit less of the global warming gas, CO_2, per mile such as LPG (Liquefied Petroleum Gas).*
- *You can now purchase dual fuel vehicles which run on both conventional fuel and LPG, ensuring that you never run out of fuel with the advantage that LPG costs about half the price of conventional fuel per litre and emits lower levels of CO_2 and other polluting gases.*
- *If you can't cycle consider buying an electric car for local journeys but only if you've already switched to a green energy supplier or if you produce your own electricity in large enough quantities.*
- *When buying a new car, ensure that it is the most environmentally friendly and fuel efficient in its range. You could reduce your CO_2 emissions and your fuel bills by up to 45 per cent per year (Honda seem to be the current market leaders in environmentally friendly, fuel-efficient cars but it's still worth researching the current market).*
- *Avoid air travel for journeys under about 500 km which generates around three times more CO_2 per passenger than rail travel.*
- *Consider a green emergency breakdown service or green car insurance and check the Internet for choices in your region.*
- *Offset your carbon emissions caused by travel, especially air travel and pay your voluntary fuel tax or join a tree planting scheme to offset your carbon emissions on a regular basis.*
- *Fit a fuel-saving device to the fuel line of your car which could save you up to 10 per cent in fuel costs and reduce emissions by up to 40 per cent.*
- *Boycott and campaign against companies such as ESSO until they change their stance on global warming and stop interfering with international negotiations to tackle climate change.*
- *Consider using a bio-fuel to power your vehicle such as jojoba, rapeseed, and sunflower or soybean oil (visit www.greenfutures.org.uk or www.lowimpact.org).*

Green parent guide to holidays and travel

🍃 Walk or use public transport as often as possible. Make sure your car is serviced as regularly as possible. Keep tyres pumped up and don't drive unnecessary weight around. Try to holiday in the UK. If holidaying abroad, pay your fuel tax to offset your carbon emissions.

🍃🍃 Invest in a bike and bike seat or hire one out and use it as much as possible. Become part of a tree replanting scheme to offset your carbon emissions. Fit a fuel-saving device to your car. If buying a new car buy a small energy-efficient model. If holidaying abroad try to book via a responsible travel agent or try a volunteer or organic holiday. Practice the same energy-saving principles abroad as you would at home and avoid purchasing drinking water in plastic bottles. Buy locally produced gifts.

🍃🍃🍃 Ditch your car completely and rely on public transport or become part of a community car share scheme. Convert your car to use bio-fuel or buy an electric car powered by renewable energy. Don't holiday abroad and if you do book an eco-holiday which supports local economies, conservation projects and cultures. Try a house swap holiday. Go camping.

14

Money matters

In this chapter you will learn:
- *how your money makes a difference*
- *how to make your money green*
- *where to get ethical investment advice.*

Money really does count! It's important to look at how we invest, save and spend our money. The number of multinational companies has jumped from 7,000 in 1970 to 45,000 today and their economic power now rivals that of many governments. Our everyday lives are affected by them but, unlike governments, they are not accountable to the general public only to shareholders and investors. Through our investments, insurance, mortgages and savings we indirectly provide businesses with large sums of money but through doing so we can also challenge their activities.

If you are planning to invest money, start a trust fund for your child or a pension, check out the ethical credentials of the companies first. Again, the Good Shopping Guide is a great source of information for this. Some companies fund military regimes or the supply of weapons, drug testing on animals and child labour. Similarly banks may be involved in activities such as funding or trade with oppressive regimes, genetic modification research or the distribution of arms so it's best to check the credentials of your bank too, choosing one with sound environmental policies, supporting local business, fair trade and renewable energy. This way your money can work for, not against the world. Every bank should be able to make a copy of their ethical policy available to you. If they can't then this is not just ethically questionable but rubbish customer care too!

Many banks also run offshore call centres, closing centres in their own country in favour of cheap labour in developing countries. While this foreign investment offers valuable income and jobs for the host country, call centre workers are often qualified to graduate standard and paid a fraction of their worth. Although their pay is good by local standards, the company employing them is making huge savings on wages compared to what they'd have to pay back in their own country. Meanwhile, thousands of valuable jobs are lost when call centres close. We all know how frustrating it is to deal with a person with a strong foreign accent on the other side of the world over a dodgy phone line. Is it really fair that this highly skilled individual should be on the receiving end of our frustration? Financial institutions, and other companies, need to be accountable for exploiting an opportunity for profit in favour of quality service and ethics.

We're constantly told that our bank, insurance or mortgage company are working for us and have our best interests at heart, but the majority of financial institutions have one objective: making money. Here are some guidelines for helping your family make their money as green as possible!

Banks and building societies

They are normally chosen as a safe place to keep our money based on loyalty, convenience and competitive interest rates but have you ever stopped to wonder what else your savings can give you? Try to support mutual building societies, excluding ones that are demutualized (they have become banks). Mutual building societies don't have shareholders so they don't have to pay out dividends. Profits can therefore be poured back into the business in the form of lower loan charges and higher interest rates for savers. Some mutual building societies don't have business customers. No commercial lending means they can't fund dubious business practices such as logging or genetic engineering research.

Many banks have been criticized for holding Third World debt. Most have now written this debt off but some haven't. It's worth checking this out with your existing bank or before opening a new account. Other things to watch out for are political donations, support for genetic engineering, factory farming, animal testing and nuclear power, oppressive regimes, environmental reporting records, pollution, workers rights and irresponsible marketing.

Make sure you know what your family's savings are being used for as well as getting the best deal on the high street. Do your homework!

Charity credit cards and affinity cards

These can help you and your family donate to your chosen charity or charities without any effort at all. As soon as you sign up for a charity credit card a donation is made to the charity and thereafter a small percentage for every £100/$200 (or similar amount) you spend goes straight to the charity. The charities benefit from the money you donate and the extra publicity they gain from the associated marketing. Very few charity credit cards charge an annual fee but it's worth checking on this before taking one out. Some have low introductory rates for the first few months after taking it out and most have rates close to the general average. However, paying off your bill in full means you won't have to pay any rates at all and it's a good habit to get into! Donations depend on the money you spend not on how big your balance is so the charity won't lose out if you keep paying off your balance. Make sure the charity card you choose is run by a bank or organization with sound policies and ethics.

Some banks are now exploring alternatives to PVC for their credit and debit cards with a view to creating a biodegradable card (made of polyethylene teraphthalate) which is also free of toxic chemicals. Ask banks and building societies what they make their cards from and if it's still PVC, urge them to change it.

Insurance companies

They keep changing, merging and taking over other companies and the deals they offer keep changing too, so it can all get a bit bewildering. One way to get the best out of your insurance company is to look at its ethical policies and find out about its investments. Insurance companies invest money in shares and although most insurers don't have an ethical investment policy, there's no harm in asking where they make their investments and putting pressure on insurers to demand more ethical behaviour from the companies they invest in.

With the freak weather conditions we have experienced recently, some insurance companies have raised premiums and withdrawn flood cover. The rate of natural disasters has been doubling every decade and requires insurers to make huge pay-outs. As a result of this threat to profits and indeed to sustainability, many insurance companies have become involved in the UN Environment Programmes Insurance Industry Initiative (UNEP) which aims to address the issues of pollution reduction, climate change and the efficient use of resources with the aim of working out more sustainable policies around the world. Make sure the insurance company you use is involved with UNEP. Look for the greener ones and the best deals at www.gooshing.co.uk.

Mortgages

This is one of the biggest investments we make in our lifetime but are our monthly repayments contributing toward loans for companies involved in activities with which we would be strongly against? A mortgage company's lending policies are as important as the rate and the kind of mortgage they offer. Try to use a bank or building society mortgage that has an ethical lending policy. Building societies are less likely than banks to be involved in questionable corporate lending. Some companies even offer a green mortgage which includes an environmental survey to assess how energy efficient your house is and what measures you can take to save energy. Others will only lend to properties which they deem to have energy-saving properties and benefits. Some attempt to encourage the renovation and restoration of old buildings for residential use and others to offset a proportion of your house's carbon emissions.

Ethical investment

This is one of the most effective ways of putting ethical consumerism into practice. Whether you're investing for your child's future or for the whole family, wouldn't you like to have the peace of mind knowing your money is benefiting not only you but also others?

As companies and investors become more aware of the benefits of ethical investment, more and more SRIs (Socially Responsible Investments) are becoming available all over the world. As well as Japan, Australia and Singapore, there are now over 280 SRIs in Europe, and so it's becoming increasingly easy to put your money where your mouth is. First identify which social, environmental or ethical issues are important to you, and then explore the range of different funds available. Check the credentials of green funds

and make sure you know what you are investing in. Contact an
information service which specializes in ethical investment
(see Taking it further section).

Child trust funds

These have been introduced in various forms in some countries as a
government incentive to help you save for your child's future. They
are basically long-term savings and investment accounts where your
child (and nobody else) can withdraw the money when they turn 18.
Neither parent nor child will pay tax on income and gains in this
type of account and state contributions to savings are made with
the birth of the child and another at a later stage. All child trust
fund providers are required to publicize their policy about social,
ethical and environmental investments, if they have one. You may
wish to ask providers about this when you are considering which
account and provider to choose. A child trust fund is basically
another type of investment so use the same guidelines for these
as for ethical investment.

Pension funds

They control a sizeable amount of the stock market so it's worth
reading the small print as one man's happy retirement could be
another's misery. Look at the fund's Statement of Investment
Principles and if you don't have a copy ask the company to send
you one. Research has shown that too many pension funds
(including local authority, union, health service and even charity
pensions) are being invested in the arms trade. Make sure this
does not include your money.

Recently we have become more interested and worried about
the deeper implications of where our money goes in the grand
corporate scheme of things, but ethical money is still a relatively

new concept so it can still be quite a trial to get to the bottom of things in an environment where complete ethical transparency is the exception rather than the rule. However, learning the financial language of the fund or investment you're dealing with will immediately give you a big advantage and help you get the most out of your financial institution on all fronts.

Alternatively, you could try forgetting money altogether! Sounds crazy but it's more widespread than you think. More and more communities are resorting to alternative money systems where they trade resources instead of money. The Local Exchange Trading Scheme (LETS) is perhaps the most well known. It promotes the exchange of goods and services so individuals, groups and businesses can function in the community without the use of money. If there's not one near you why not start your own? Visit www.newciv.org/ncn/moneyteam.html or www.letslinkuk.org for more information.

Green parenting guide to money matters

💧 Try to use organizations that don't use overseas call centres. Use a charity credit card.

💧💧 Bank with an ethical bank. If switching to one tell your old bank exactly why you are moving your custom and ask them to take action. Likewise, make sure savings for your child are with an institution whose ethical policies you agree with. Check out where your pension, insurance and mortgage money is being invested.

💧💧💧 Bank ethically, invest ethically, take out a green mortgage, join a LETS scheme, and lobby financial institutions to change their ethics.

The whole package

In this chapter you will learn:
- *how to incorporate what you've learned in this book into a modern lifestyle*
- *how to avoid overwhelming yourself*
- *how to approach green parenting holistically.*

As you can see the whole subject of green parenting is huge and it doesn't stop here. There are a number of other subjects that you could look into, such as green weddings and celebrations, green dating agencies, going green at work or finding a green job and green eco-friendly burials. As time goes on it'll be much easier to access information and services to choose a more ethical and environmentally friendly way of life as governments introduce more and more measures for climate control and energy saving. In time it'll become a habit for everyone, but in the meantime try to do what you can in your own small way. It may seem like a bit of an awkward lifestyle change at first, but by making small changes now you'll hardly notice the difference later.

Being a green parent isn't just about what you can practically do as a family to lessen your impact on the environment and vulnerable cultures or economies. It's also about your attitude to life in general. If your aim in life is to make lots of cash so you can have as many material possessions as possible and are willing to stick the kids in nursery every day and work every hour god gives in order to achieve this, then perhaps green parenting is not for you. In order to teach your family about their environment and how to harmonize with it and respect it, even in the smallest ways, it's important to spend quality time together as a family. Take time out to explore all aspects of green parenting together and learn how to perhaps live life a little bit slower. After all, what's the point of having lots of money and possessions and no time to use them? Who wants to look back on their life and wish they'd spent more time with the kids as they grew up? Work–life balance is an important element of being a green parent. With a little careful consideration, communication, budgeting and planning you can prioritize a more fulfilling work–life balance for you and your family. If you'd like more information on helping to prioritize your needs and achieving balance in your life, www.authentictransformation.co.uk is a really helpful site.

Family, close friends and your involvement with your community also help form a solid foundation for managing a healthy work–life balance and support and understanding for a greener lifestyle. We often live in our own self-contained worlds with little quality time spent with ourselves or others. Family, friends and community all help to share burdens, thoughts and ideas and make our green aspirations realities. Elderly members of our families are mines of valuable advice and information who are so often overlooked or seen as a burden but they are also a vital link in your family circle. From babysitting pools and sharing a box scheme to community LETS and recycling, your friends, family and community are your support network so try get involved, no matter how small your contribution. Remember that there is more strength in numbers!

Relationships between parents are also extremely important whether living together or apart. Try to set out clear and simple shared values not only about your green priorities and any lifestyle changes you'd like to make but also about your emotional needs and communication. Take time to talk with each other and don't be shy about using different communication techniques or even getting help if things get tricky. Ensuring that we each take a little time out each day to be quiet and alone allows us to gather our thoughts and be more productive within our relationships too.

You're probably thinking it all sounds great but how do I realistically fit in green parenting with the demands and priorities of a modern lifestyle? It can sometimes feel like it's more hassle than it's worth as our consumer-led society continues to put pressures and anxieties on us to conform. Remind yourself of the benefits. If you're feeling a bit overwhelmed by it all, take a deep breath and go back through the chapters using the Green Parent Guide to help you prioritize what's important to you for each subject. Write them down and then beside them make a note of how you and your family can accommodate each change into your life. Start with easy ones first and once they've become a habitual part of your lifestyle, introduce slightly more difficult ones. If those work, then you can go the all the way and introduce your whole package. Focus on the benefits that a green lifestyle can bring to your family and when it's all in place you can have a good old gloat to yourself about how green you and your family are!

Don't worry if some things don't work out. At least you tried. Ask around and find out if anyone can help you with other ideas or practical solutions. This is a great way to get involved with your community and strengthen bonds within it too.

Only take on what is financially and reasonably practical for your lifestyle and try to make the changes fun. Martyring yourself to the cause will only make you resent your new lifestyle and simple green changes will become a chore. Remember, going green is for everyone.

Top 5 green parenting tips

1 *Breastfeed.*
2 *Use cloth nappies.*
3 *Eat fresh (organic) food where possible.*
4 *Save energy where possible.*
5 *Buy local and ditch the supermarket!*

Many people are still quite reluctant to change old habits but with time they'll realize that just as attitudes to smoking have changed, attitudes to the environment will too and they'll be swept along with everyone else. Why not get ahead of the crowd and start implementing these changes sooner rather than later? Just think of the money you'll save.

If you have been truly inspired by this book and are about to go off, buy a plot of land and build your very own earthship eco-build or start a yoga retreat, great, please get in touch and let us know about it! You'll find lots of useful resources in the next section. Otherwise, good luck to you and your family for a beautiful, healthy, environmentally friendly future. Remember, prioritize and keep it simple!

Happy green parenting.

Taking it further

Hopefully this book has been useful to you by giving you a comprehensive outline with hints and tips about how to be a green parent. However there is always more to learn. Regulations, services and advice vary from country to country so it's important to make sure you check out the situation in your own country, state or region.

If you'd like to further your knowledge about any of the issues covered in this book, the recommendations in this chapter will hopefully help you find what you need or at least point you in the right direction!

Useful organizations

BIRTH AND PREGNANCY

Active Birth Centre
25 Bickerton Road
London
N19 5JT
Tel: 020 7281 6760
www.activebirthcentre.com

American College of Nurse Midwives
818 Connecticut Avenue
Washington
DC 20006
Tel: 001 202 728 9860
www.acnm.org

International Caesarean Awareness Network
1304 Kingsdale Avenue
Redondo Beach
CA 90278
Tel: 001 800 686 4226
www.ican-online.org

Midwives Alliance of North America
611 Pennsylvania Avenue
SE 1700
Washington DC
20003–4303
Tel: 001 888 923 6262
www.mana.org

American Association of Birth Centers
3123 Gottschall Road
Perkiomenville
PA 18074
Tel: 001 215 234 8068
www.birthcenters.org

National Childbirth Trust (NCT)
Alexandra House
Oldham Terrace
London
W3 6NH
Tel: 0870 444 8707
www.nct.org.uk

BREASTFEEDING

Association of Breastfeeding Mothers
PO Box 207
Bridgwater
Somerset

TA6 7YT
Tel: 0870 401 7711
www.abm.me.uk

Breastfeeding Network
PO Box 11126
Paisley
PA2 8YB
Tel: 0870 900 8787
www.breastfeedingnetwork.org

La Leche League GB
PO Box 29
West Bridgford
Nottingham
NG2 7NP
Tel: 0845 120 2918
www.lalecheleague.org

CLOTHES AND ACCESSORIES

Clean Slate
Organic and ethical school uniform supplier.
www.cleanslateclothing.co.uk

COMPLEMENTARY MEDICINE AND HEALTH

Autism Medical
www.autismmedical.com

BCMA (The British Complementary Medicine Association)
PO Box 5122
Bournemouth
BH8 0WG
Tel: 0845 345 5977
www.bcma.co.uk

British Allergy Foundation (Allergy UK)
3 White Oak Square
London Road
Swanley
Kent
BR8 7AG
Tel: 01322 619898
www.allergyuk.org

British Medical Acupuncture Society
BMAS House
3 Winnington Court
Northwich
Cheshire
CW8 1AQ
Tel: 01606 786782
www.medical-acupuncture.co.uk

British Osteopathic Association
Langham House West
Mill Street
Luton
LU1 2NA
Tel: 01582 488455
www.osteopathy.org

Asthma UK
Summit House
70 Wilson Street
London
EC2A 2DB
Tel: 020 786 4900
www.asthma.org.uk

National Eczema Society
Hill House
Highgate Hill
London

N19 5NA
Tel: 0870 241 3604
www.eczema.org

National Institute of Medical Herbalists
Elm House
54 Mary Arches Street
Exeter
EX4 3BA
Tel: 01392 426022
www.nimh.org.uk

Society of Homeopaths
11 Brookfield
Duncan Close
Moulton Park Industrial Estate
Northampton
NN3 6WL
Tel: 0845 450 6611
www.homeopathy-soh.org

The Cranialsacral Therapy Association
Monomark House
27 Old Gloucester Street
London
WC1N 3XX
Tel: 0700 0784 785
www.craniosacral.co.uk

The Guild of Infant and Child Massage
22 Elder Close
Uttoxeter
Staffs
ST14 8UR
Tel: 01889 564555
www.gicm.org.uk

ENERGY

National Energy Foundation
Free advice from a UK charity on energy efficiency.
Davy Avenue
Knowlhill
Milton Keynes
MK5 8NG
Tel: 01908 665555
www.nef.org.uk

ENVIRONMENTAL

Forest Stewardship Council
11–13 Great Oak Street
Llanidloes
Powys
SY18 6BU
Tel: 01686 413916
www.fscus.org

Women's Environmental Network
PO Box 30626
London
E1 1TZ
Tel: 020 7481 9004
www.wen.org.uk

FAIR TRADE

Fairtrade Foundation
Room 204
16 Baldwin's Green
London
EC1N 7RJ
Tel: 020 7405 5942
www.fairtrade.org.uk

FOOD

Baby Milk Action
23 St Andrew's Street
Cambridge
CB2 3AX
Tel: 01223 464420
www.babymilkaction.org

Food Standards Agency
All the information on organic food, food safety and GM crops.
www.foodstandards.gov.uk

HOLIDAYS AND TRAVEL

Environmental Transport Association (ETA)
Campaigning for a sustainable transport system.
68 High Street
Weybridge
KT13 8RS
Tel: 01932 828882
www.eta.co.uk

International Centre for Responsible Tourism
School of Science
University of Greenwich
Medway University Campus
Pembroke
Chatham Maritime
Kent
ME4 4TB
www.icrtourism.org

Sustrans (Safe Routes to Schools Team)
National Cycle Network Centre
2 Cathedral Square
College Green

Bristol
BS1 5DD
Tel: 0117 915 0100
www.sustrans.org.uk

Tourism Concern
Stapleton House
277–81 Holloway Road
London
N7 8HN
Tel: 020 7133 3330
www.tourismconcern.org.uk

HOME

Environmental Building News
122 Bierge Street
Brattleboro
VT 05301
Tel: 001 802 257 7300
www.buildinggreen.com

MONEY

Ethical Investment Research Service (EIRIS)
Research into corporate behaviour for ethical investors.
80–4 Bondway
London
SW8 1SF
Tel: 020 7840 5700
www.eiris.org

Triodos Bank
A European ethical bank.
Brunel House
11 The Promenade
Bristol

BS8 3NN
Tel: 01179 739399
www.triodos.co.uk

NAPPIES

Nappy Lady
Advice and information on all aspects of swapping to real nappies.
16 Hill Brow
Bearstead
Maidstone
Kent
ME14 4 AW
Tel: 0845 456 2441
www.thenappylady.co.uk

ORGANIC

Organic Consumers Association
6771 South Silver Hill Drive
Finland MN55603
Tel: 00 358 218 226 4164
www.organicconsumers.org

Organic Trade Association
PO Box 1078
Greenfield
MA 01301
Tel: 001 413 774 7511
www.ota.com

Soil Association
Bristol House
40–56 Victoria Street
Bristol
BS1 6BY
Tel: 0117 314 5000
www.whyorganic.org

PARENTING

BabyGROE
112–14 Main Street
Lochgelly
Fife
KY11 1JW
Tel: 01592 784700
www.babygroe.co.uk

Connexions
Offers advice and support for young people aged 13–19 throughout
England. Call this number to find support in your local area.
Tel: 080 800 13 2 19 (Helpline)
www.connexions-direct.com

Gingerbread
Offers advice on any issues regarding being a lone parent.
307 Borough High Street
London
SE1 1JH
Tel: 0800 018 4318
www.gingerbread.org.uk

Home Start
2 Salisbury Road
Leicester
LE1 7QR
Tel: 0800 068 6368
www.home-start.org.uk

Hyperactive Children's Support Group
71 Whyke Lane
Chichester
West Sussex
PO19 2LD
Tel: 01243 539966
www.hacsg.org.uk

SHOPPING

British Association of Fair Trade Shops
Unit 7
8–13 New Inn Street
London
EC2A 3PY
Tel: 07796 050045
www.bafts.org.uk

Buy Recycled
A guide to products available in the UK containing
recycled materials.
www.recycledproducts.org.uk

Ethical Consumer
Unit 21
41 Old Birley Street
Manchester
M15 5RF
Tel: 0161 226 2929
www.ethicalconsumer.org

Green Choices
PO Box 31617
London
SW2 4FF
www.greenchoices.org

Green Matters
www.greenmatters.com

Local Exchange Trading System
Community-based networks linking people with goods
to swap and trade.
www.letslinkuk.net

Useful websites

BIRTH AND PREGNANCY

Birthpartners.com
Database to search for doulas, midwives and all aspects of
pregnancy and birthing.
www.birthpartners.com

Birth Works
www.birthworks.org

Childbirth.org
Massive database and links to many aspects of childbirth and
pregnancy.
www.childbirth.org

Doula Association
www.doula.org.uk

Doulas of North America
www.dona.com

Foresight
Pre-conceptual care.
www.foresight-preconception.org.uk

Fertility UK
National Fertility Awareness and Natural Family Planning Service.
www.fertilityuk.org

Gentlewater
Information on Water Birth.
www.gentlewater.co.uk

Home Birth
www.homebirth.org.uk

International Childbirth Education Association
www.icea.org

Sheila Kitzinger
Website of author and all-round expert.
www.sheilakitzinger.com

BREASTFEEDING

Association of Breastfeeding Mothers
www.abm.me.uk

UNICEF Baby Friendly Initiative
www.babyfriendly.org.uk

TOILETRIES AND COSMETICS

Beauty Without Cruelty
www.bwcv.com

Cosmetic, Toiletry and Perfumery Association
www.ctpa.org.uk

Chemical Body Burden
Information on bio-accumulative synthetic material.
www.chemicalbodyburden.org

EPA
US Environmental Protection Agency.
www.epa.gov

Making Cosmetics
How to make your own from natural raw materials.
www.makingcosmetic.com

Marshmallow
Tips on making your own cosmetic products.
www.marshmallow.co.uk

Not Too Pretty
Information on cosmetics and associated products that contain phthalates.
www.nottoopretty.org

SAFEMINDS
Information on mercury-based neurological conditions founded by parents of children who have been affected.
www.safeminds.org

COMPLEMENTARY MEDICINE AND HEALTH

Allergymatters
www.allergymatters.com

American Holistic Health Association
www.ahha.org

Association of Reflexologists
www.reflexology.org

21st Century Health
www.21stcenturyhealth.co.uk

European College of Bowen Studies
www.thebowentechnique.co.uk

Global Vaccine Awareness League
www.gval.com

Femcare Plus
Healthy, safe and environmentally sound feminine hygiene products.
www.femininehygiene.com

International Federation of Aromatherapists
www.ifaroma.org

National Asthma Campaign
www.asthma.org.uk

National Vaccine Information Center
US-based vaccine information network.
www.909shot.com

The Informed Parent
www.informedparent.co.uk

ENERGY

Energy Star
Information on energy saving and the energy saving star rating.
www.energystar.gov

Energy Saving Trust
Promoting sustainable energy in the UK.
www.est.org.uk

Green Batteries
Promoting the use of rechargable batteries.
www.greenbatteries.com

Green Energy
Encouraging sustainable and renewable energy resources.
www.greenenergy.org.uk

Office of Energy Efficiency and Renewable Energy
Bringing the future of energy to children.
www.eere.energy.gov

Save Energy
All about saving energy in the home.
www.energysavingtrust.org.uk

Solar Twin Ltd.
Solar panel information and supplier.
www.solartwin.com

Use Less Energy
www.uselessenergy.org.uk

ENVIRONMENTAL

Best Foot Forward
A variety of tools to help assess ecological footprint.
www.bestfootforward.com

Carbon Calculator
www.carboncalculator.com

Centre for Alternative Technology
www.cat.org.uk

Compassion in World Farming
www.ciwf.org

Earthwatch Institute
International environmental charity.
www.earthwatch.org

Eden Project
Information, education and research into the huge Cornwall bio-domes.
www.edenproject.com

EM Radiation Research Trust
Information arising from the debate on the effects of electromagnetic radiation.
www.radiationresearch.org

Environment Agency
Information on how to save water.
www.environment-agency.gov.uk

Environmental Investigation Agency
www.eia-international.org

Friends of the Earth
www.foei.org

Global Action Plan
www.globalactionplan.org.uk

Greenpeace
www.greenpeace.org.uk

International Tree Foundation
www.internationaltreefoundation.org

Sitefinder Mobile Phone Base Station Database
www.sitefinder.ofcom.gov.uk

The Carbon Trust
Free advice on how to reduce carbon emissions.
www.carbontrust.co.uk

The Environment Trust
www.envirotrust.org

The Marine Stewardship Council
www.msc.org

The National Trust
www.nationaltrust.org.uk

The Rainforest Foundation
www.rainforestfoundationuk.org

Wastewatch
www.wastewatch.org.uk

Woodland Trust
Protecting the native woodland of the UK.
www.woodland-trust.org.uk

World Wildlife Fund
www.wwf-uk.org

FAIR TRADE

Ethical Consumer
www.ethicalconsumer.org

Oxfam
www.oxfam.org.uk

Sweat Shop Watch
www.sweatshopwatch.org

The Fairtrade Foundation
www.fairtrade.org.uk

FATHERS

Families Need Fathers
www.fnf.org.uk

Fathers Direct
The national information centre on fatherhood.
www.fathersdirect.com

Fathers Journal
True and reflective writings from real dads.
www.fathersjournal.com

FOOD

EOSTA
Global organic and biodynamic fruit and vegetable distribution.
www.eosta.com

Henry Doubleday Research Association
Promoting organic farming and food.
www.gardenorganic.org.uk

McSpotlight
Facts, figures and history of McDonald's and the McLibel cases.
www.mcspotlight.org

National Association of Farmers Markets
www.farmersmarkets.net

Organic Food, UK
All the news and views on organic food.
www.organicfoodee.com

Slow Food Movement
Promoting the antidote to fast food.
www.slowfood.com

The Food Commission
www.foodcomm.org.uk

The Green Guide Online
Environmental update on food and much more.
www.greenguideonline.com

Vegan Society
www.vegansociety.com

Vegetarian Society
www.vegsoc.org

HOLIDAYS AND TRAVEL

Country Lovers
Information on visiting the UK countryside.
www.countrylover.co.uk

Ecovolunteer
Information on trips to worldwide conservation destinations.
www.ecovolunteer.org.uk

Ethical Escape
Database of worldwide ethical holiday destinations.
www.ethicalescape.com

Ethical Traveler
Global network of travellers and ethical tourist agencies.
www.ethicaltraveler.org

Exodus Travels
All things ethical in holidays.
www.exodus.co.uk

Explore Worldwide
Ethical adventure holidays around the world.
www.exploreworldwide.com

Festival Eye
Listing of all major festivals, camps and other UK outdoor events.
www.festivaleye.com

Free Wheelers
Campaign to reduce car-based pollution.
www.freewheelers.com

Hiking Website
Make the most of hiking with gear, trails and more.
www.hikingwebsite.com

Hostels.com
Worldwide hostel database.
www.hostels.com

Responsibletravel.com
Promoting eco-tourism worldwide.
www.responsibletravel.com

School Run
Organization linking parents to share the school-run duties.
www.school-run.org

The Ramblers Association
www.ramblers.org.uk

UK Attractions
www.uk-tourist-attractions.co.uk

Willing Workers on Organic Farms (WWOOF)
Information on volunteering on organic farms around the globe.
www.wwoof.org

HOME

Association for Environment Concious Building
Campaigning for more environmental awareness in the
building industry.
www.aecb.net

Construction Resources
Information on ecological building materials.
www.constructionresources.com

Denes Natural Pet Care
Holistic pet care organization.
www.denes.com

E-Cloths
www.e-cloth.com

Green Building Store
Energy-efficient home materials supplier.
www.greenbuildingstore.co.uk

Green Pest Co
Environmentally friendly ways to rid your home of unwanted pests.
www.greenpestco.com

Low Impact Living Initiative
www.lowimpact.org

RSPCA
www.rspca.org.uk

The Blue Cross
Advice and support on keeping pets and horses ethically.
www.bluecross.org.uk

The New Homemaker
www.thenewhomemaker.com

MONEY

Ethical Investors Group
50 per cent of profits go to specific charities.
www.ethicalinvestors.co.uk

Ethical Wills
www.ethicalwill.com

NAPPIES

National Association of Nappy Services
Increasing awareness and promoting the use of real nappies.
www.changeanappy.co.uk

WRAP Real Nappy Helpline
www.realnappycampaign.com

ORGANIC

Green Choices
The green living guide.
www.greenchoices.org

Organic Consumers' Association
Campaigning for all aspects of organic lifestyles.
www.organicconsumers.org

Pesticide Action Network
www.pan-uk.org

Plants for a Future
Permaculture, edible and medicinal plants.
www.PFAF.org

PARENTING

Attachment Parenting International
www.attachmentparenting.org

CRY-SYS
Support and advice for parents of crying babies.
www.cry-sis.org.uk

Parents, Families and Friends of Lesbians and Gays (PFLAG)
www.pflag.org

PLAY AND EDUCATION

Education Otherwise
Home education information and database.
www.education-otherwise.org

Green Books
A range of books on environmental subjects.
www.greenbooks.co.uk

Institute for Play
Championing the benefits of play for kids and adults.
www.instituteforplay.com

Woodcraft Folk
Games, drama, crafts and education for youngsters.
www.woodcraft.org.uk

RECYCLING

Cartridge World
Find your nearest recycling facility with a postcode search.
www.cartridgeworld.org

Community Composting Network
www.communitycompost.org

Composting Toilet World
www.compostingtoilet.org

Freecycle
Direct recycling: give unwanted things to other people.
www.freecycle.org

Green Metropolis
Online bookshop for trading second-hand books.
www.greenmetropolis.com

Ollie Recycles
The new three Rs for children: reduce, reuse and recycle.
www.ollierecycles.com/uk

Preloved
Buy and sell second-hand items.
www.preloved.co.uk

Recoup
www.recoup.org

The Composting Association
Fact and figures on composting.
www.compost.org.uk

The Natural Death Centre
Charity offering support on natural burials.
www.naturaldeath.org.uk

SHOPPING

Gooshing
Price search facility and ethical comparison site.
www.gooshing.co.uk

No Sweat
Campaigning against the use of sweatshops in manufacturing.
www.nosweat.org.uk

Further reading

BIRTH AND PREGNANCY

Balsakas, J. *New Natural Pregnancy: Practical Well-being from Conception to Birth* (Interlink, 1999).

Cheatham, K. *Childbirth Education for Women with Disabilities and Their Partners* (International Childbirth Education Association, 1994).

Daniels, K. *The Water Baby Information Book* (Point of View Productions, 1988).

Kitzinger, S. *The Complete Book of Pregnancy and Childbirth* (AA Knopf, 1996).

Korte, D. *The VBAC Companion: The Expectant Mother's Guide to Vaginal Birth after Caesarean* (Harvard Common Press, 1997).

Odent, M. *Primal Health* (Century Hutchinson, 1986).

Odent, M. *Birth Reborn* (Fontana, 1986).

Marti, J; Heather, B. *Holistic Pregnancy and Childbirth: A Month-by-Month Guide* (J. Wiley and Sons, 1999).

Motha, Dr. G. *The Gentle Birth Method* (Swan MacLeod, 2004).

O'Mara, Peggy (ed); Ponte, W. *Having a Baby, Naturally: The Mothering Magazine Guide to Pregnancy and Childbirth* (Atria Books, 2003).

Rogers, J; Matsumura, M. *Mothers to Be: A Guide to Pregnancy and Birth for Women with Disabilities* (Demos, 1991).

Wesson, N. *Enhancing Fertility Naturally: Holistic Therapies for a Successful Pregnancy* (Healing Arts Press, 1999).

BREASTFEEDING

Adamson, E; Kays, M. *Breastfeeding: a Holistic Handbook* (Berkely, 1999).

Trotter, S. *Breastfeeding: The Essential Guide* (Trotters Independent Publishing Services Ltd, 2004).

COMPLEMENTARY MEDICINE AND HEALTH

Balaskas, J. and A. *New Life: The Exercise Book for Childbirth* (Sidgwick and Jackson, 1983).

Castro, M. *The Complete Homoeopathy Handbook* (St. Martin's, 1990).

Cave, S. *What Your Doctors May Not Tell You about Children's Vaccinations: Hidden Dangers, Pros and Cons, and Safety Measures That Can Protect Your Child* (Warner Books, 2001).

Dale, B and Roebar, J. *Exercise for Childbirth* (Century, 1982).

Hoffmann, D. *The Complete Illustrated Holistic Herbal: A Safe and Practical Guide to Making and Using Herbal Remedies* (Element Books, 1996).

Offit, P. *What Every Parent Should Know about Vaccines* (Macmillan, 1998).

Romm, A. J. *Vaccinations: A Thoughtful Parents Guide – How to make Safe, Sensible Decisions about the Risks, Benefits and Alternatives* (Healing Arts Press, 2001).

Walker, P. *Baby Massage* (Bloomsbury, 1998).

FATHERS AND PARTNERS

Heinowitz, J. *Fathering Right From the Start: Straight Talk about Pregnancy, Birth and Beyond* (New World Library, 2001).

Jones, C. and Jones, J. *The Birth Partners Handbook* (Meadowbrook Press, 1989).

Jones, C; Henci, G; Simkin, P. *The Labour Support Guide: For Fathers, Family and Friends* (International Childbirth Education Association, 1984).

Pruett, K. *The Nurturing Father: Journey Toward the Complete Man* (Warner, 1987).

Roebar, J. *Shared Parenthood – A Handbook for Fathers* (Century, 1987).

FOOD

Johnson, R. (ed) *Whole Foods for the Whole Family* (La Leche League International, 1993).

Lappe, F. M. *Diet for a Small Planet* (Ballantine, 1991).

Onstad, D. *Whole Foods Companion: A Guide for Adventurous Cooks, Curious Shoppers & Lovers of Natural Food* (Chelsea Green Publishing, 1996).

Yntema, S. *Vegetarian Pregnancy: The Definitive Nutritional Guide to Having a Healthy Baby* (McBooks Press, 1996).

HOME

Bourne, J; Jones, E. (ed) *Go Mad Go Make a Difference 2: Over 500 Daily Ways to Save the Planet (Think Publishing, 2003)*.

McCarthy, D. *Saving the Planet Without Costing the Earth: 500 Simple Steps to a Greener Lifestyle* (Fusion Press, 2004).

ORGANIC

Maxted-Frost, T. *The Organic Baby Book* (Green Books, 2003).

PARENTING

Balaskas, J. *Natural Baby: How to Optimize Your Child's Development in the First Year of Life* (Gaia Books, 2001).

Liedloff, J. *The Continuum Concept* (Futura, 1976).

SHOPPING

Sankey, W. (ed) *The Good Shopping Guide* (Ethical Company Organization, 2005).

Index